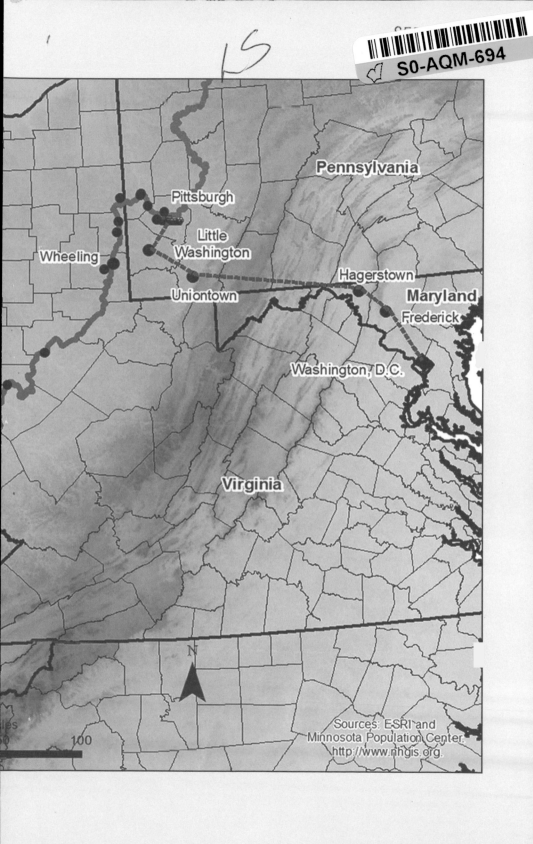

Pennsylvania

Pittsburgh

Little
Washington

Wheeling

Uniontown

Hagerstown

Maryland

Frederick

Washington, D.C.

Virginia

N

Sources: ESRI and
Minnesota Population Center.
http://www.nhgis.org.

100

Bittersweet JOURNEY

Bittersweet JOURNEY

Andrew Jackson's
1829 Inaugural Trip

CARLTON JACKSON

Acclaim Press
MORLEY, MISSOURI

Acclaim Press
— Your Next Great Book —

P.O. Box 238
Morley, MO 63767
(573) 472-9800
www.acclaimpress.com

Book Design: Tiffany Glastetter
Cover Design: M. Frene Melton
Cover Sketch of Andrew Jackson: Dan Jackson
Cover Map: Debra Kreitzer, Department of Geography and Geology, Western Kentucky
    University
Artist/Illustrator: Patrick Stephen Berry
Photo of the Author: Catherine Osborne

Library of Congress Cataloging-in-Publication Data

Jackson, Carlton.
  Bittersweet journey : Andrew Jackson's inaugural trip, 1829 / by Carlton
Jackson.
      p. cm.
  ISBN-13: 978-1-935001-61-4 (alk. paper)
  ISBN-10: 1-935001-61-2 (alk. paper)
  1. Jackson, Andrew, 1767-1845--Inauguration, 1829. 2. Jackson, Andrew,
1767-1845--Travel--Washington (D.C.) 3. Jackson, Andrew,
1767-1845--Travel--Ohio River. 4. Jackson, Andrew,
1767-1845--Travel--Cumberland River (Ky. and Tenn.) I. Title.
  E382.J127 2011
  973.5'6092--dc22

                                2010037837

First Printing: 2011
Printed in the United States of America
10 9 8 7 6 5 4 3 2 1

CONTENTS

This book is lovingly dedicated to my dear sister, Vernell. And to the memory of Elvie, Lois, Pearl, Robert, James, Jean and Vondie.

INTRODUCTION

Dozens, if not hundreds, of biographies have been written about Andrew Jackson, Seventh President of the United States. The majority tell about his election in 1828 and then jump quickly to his Oath of Office in early 1829. Only a few sketchily mention the three-week trip he made between January 19 and February 11, 1829 to get to the seat of government.

He boarded a steamer at Hermitage Landing on the Cumberland River, a mile or so from his residence. Few biographies relate the places he passed through on his way to the capital city. He traveled down the Cumberland to its juncture with the Ohio River, which he followed all the way to Pittsburgh, with stops in between at such places as Smithland, Louisville, and Maysville, in Kentucky; Cincinnati in Ohio; Wheeling in Virginia; and Pittsburgh in Pennsylvania. From the latter city he traveled overland through Washington, Uniontown, and Brownsville, in Pennsylvania; and Hagerstown and Frederick in Maryland, on into Washington City. At all these places a majority of people treated him with respect and adoration; the inhabitants of a few places, however, made it clear that the sooner Jackson left town, the better.

He and his wife, Rachel, had decided early on to leave the Hermitage on December 24, 1828, and leisurely make their way to the capital. Sadly, Christmas Eve, 1828, was the day Rachel Jackson was buried at the Hermitage. A heartbroken President-elect had to make this long journey without the company of the woman he loved.

A word or two about politics and party affiliations: Jackson was elected in 1828 through the efforts of Committees—one in Nashville, the other in Washington—that called themselves "Jackson Men." It was only while he was President that he joined the newly formed Democratic Party, the founding of which was largely the work of Jackson's second Vice-President, Martin Van

Buren. Likewise, the word "Whig," though long in use, especially in England, did not come to mean "anti-Jacksonian" until 1834 and the "war" over re-chartering the Bank of the United States.

An "overlapping theme" of this work is Irony: and tragic irony, at that. The famous as well as the unknown, along with the rich and poor, are all subject to these "laws" of Irony; life can be capricious. Quite frequently, the "best laid" plans are interrupted or changed by unforeseen circumstances. In such instances, one has to perform duties and responsibilities regardless of how much sorrow is in one's heart. Andrew Jackson, soon to become the most powerful man in America in early 1829, proved no exception to this "rule."

Another "overarching theme" of my study is that the United States was just beginning to experience a transportation revolution at the outset of Andrew Jackson's presidency. The age of the steamboat had, in fact, started only a few years before Jackson made his historic journey to Washington. When his presidency ended in 1837, railroads were making vast and rapid advances throughout the country, advances that cut considerably into stage and steamboat travel.

A third "overlapping" theme deals with what can accurately be called a "communication revolution." Samuel F.B. Morse was developing his "Morse Code" while Jackson was President; although Morse's message of "What Hath God Wrought" (1844) was spoken after Jackson's presidency, the system of telegraphy was in its formative stages while Jackson was in the White House. During this same general period, photography was in its infant stages, represented primarily by a Frenchman named Louis Daguerre. Jackson, along with John Quincy Adams, was one of the earliest presidents to be "photographed."

Most of the hazards faced by Andrew Jackson and his traveling companions have in our own day and time been alleviated. The shoals at Harpeth on the Cumberland are easily traversed today, while the Falls of the Ohio are now by-passed by the Portland Canal. Ironically, perhaps, today there is not the amount of steamboat passenger travel as there was in Jackson's time.

Passenger travel on rivers is primarily confined to day tours, tourist gambling excursions, and the like. It would be impossible today to take the same river journey that Jackson experienced in 1829. Any traffic on rivers today—not just the Cumberland and Ohio—but waterways throughout the country is almost completely confined to barges and other freight carriers. Passenger services have, of course, been taken over in succession by trains, automobiles, and airplanes.

The other major forms of Jackson's transportation have been superseded: The coach is long gone from America, and passenger trains have been sharply curtailed except for the most populated areas of the country. The eastern and western seaboards are well served by passenger trains (Amtrak), but large swathes of the very route Jackson followed to Washington are totally without trains, the "iron horses" that transport human beings.

What, then, does Jackson's journey "say" to us here in the first part of the Twenty-First Century? First and foremost, it tells us that if we want to understand the present and, hopefully, make educated guesses about the future, we need to know our past. We need to know that every form of transportation that so far has been declared a "revolution" has been either greatly modified or has passed out of existence. Steamboats, coaches, and passenger trains, in their turn, reached obsolescence; with continued oil crises, who is to say that automobile and air traffic will not be seriously altered in the years ahead? New forms of transportation have characterized much of our history, and no good reason exists to say that this "evolution" has ended.

In this book I am primarily telling a story; I do not argue a thesis. I am well aware that Andrew Jackson was, in his own time, and in fact, ours as well, a controversial figure. Many historians defend him as the harbinger of democracy as it evolved within the framework of the Constitution. Others condemn his "Indian Removal" policies, his support of slavery, and his destruction of the Bank of the United States. In this book I am trying to steer clear of these debates: I am first and foremost interested in his journey to Washington City in 1829 and then, briefly, his return to the Hermitage in 1837, after he had finished his presidency.

When I first began work on this subject, I intended it for young adult audiences. I was hoping that I could get readers 16 to 25 interested in my work on Andrew Jackson's great and melancholy journey of 1829. As the project continued, my thoughts were that it should be suitable not only for young adults but for the general reader as well. Maybe high school and college students can benefit from reading it, as well as classroom teachers and college and university professors. As far as I can tell, my reconstruction of Jackson's Inaugural Journey adds new material to the body of literature about the Seventh President of the United States, and I believe it is the first book of its kind to be found anywhere.

I have tried to make this book both narrative and interpretive, and I believe I have struck a balance between the two. As we all know, there must first be narration before there can be meaningful analysis. Interpretation without factual information behind it is not a historical study; my book on Andrew Jackson, I believe, is a historical account of a major event in the life of the Seventh President, and by extension, the country he served.

Carlton Jackson
Butler County, Kentucky
2011

Bittersweet JOURNEY

Andrew Jackson's
1829 Inaugural Trip

Andrew kneeling at Rachel's grave.

Chapter 1

DEPARTURE

Having just returned from the back of his big house where he cut four shoots of a willow tree and placed them beside a freshly-dug mound of earth,[1] the old gentleman, now a bit winded, walked slowly but firmly-with still a faint military bearing-toward his living room door, which opened out onto a spacious front yard. Two young assistants offered to hold his arms and guide him to his destination, but in his high-pitched voice with a Carolina twang to it, he politely refused.

Dressed somberly, he wore black pants and coat, a white shirt, a black armband, and a black netted cloth attached to his tall beaver hat hung low over his neck and onto his shoulders. Known as a "weeper," the cloth showed everyone in his presence that he was in mourning for an irredeemable loss. Lean in appearance, he stood six feet one inches tall and weighed 145 pounds. His hair was cropped, mostly gray now, but enough color to show that he had been a vigorous redhead in his youth. His sallow complexion's seeming fragility belied his inner strength. His strong cheekbones formed into a "lantern" jaw accentuated by a straight nose and "Grecian" mouth.[2] Though "rounded in shoulders," he stood "gracefully erect," with a deep brow and bright blue eyes that provided the keys to his disposition; they could glare, showing anger and sadness, or sparkle with delight and happiness.[3] On this occasion, they failed to sparkle.

Once he got outside his living room, standing on the porch, he saw that his entire driveway was filled with hundreds of persons who had come to see him off on the long journey ahead.

He began to walk toward his waiting coach, took off his hat, and turned around to his house, and bowed low, "as though to a lady," one person remarked.[4] Tears filled his eyes, and some in the crowd thought he might just go back into the house and forego the impending travel. Such a thought, however, never entered his mind; it would have been an abomination to the memory of the woman he had always held most dear.

Charles, one of his "servants" (a euphemism for slave) sat, waiting in the coach's driver's seat, wanting to start the four gray horses on their way. His household "servants" lined the driveway, with Hannah and Uncle Alfred, being the most noticeable, for their loud weeping. They bade "Marse Hickory" goodbye, not quite believing him when he kept saying, "I'll be back, children, I'll be back; take care of things for me."

Finally, he entered the coach and gave the signal to start on the way. Thousands of onlookers who had walked, ridden horses, come in buckboard wagons, as well as fancy coaches, to see him off on this first leg of a momentous journey packed the roadsides. A newspaper later reported that, "no man ever carried with him more truly the good wishes of his neighbors."[5]

They rode for about a mile and a half and came to a place on the Cumberland River, generally known as "Hermitage Landing." There, the gentleman stepped out of the coach while his baggage was hauled aboard a steamboat named Fairy, which had come up from Nashville the night before. When the gentleman himself walked up to the vessel, he was "piped" aboard; Captain Henry Harrison gave him a snappy salute and the entire crew was on deck, standing at attention. He received the best cabin the boat could offer.

The gentleman was Andrew Jackson, and he was on his way to Washington City, the nation's capital, to become the seventh President of the United States.

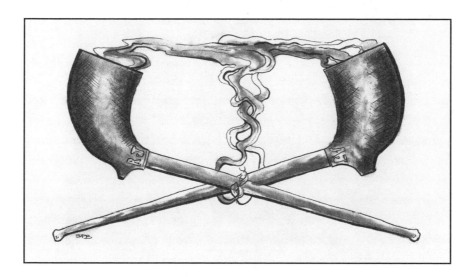

Rachel

Chapter 2

A TRAGIC IRONY

As the coach slowly made its way to the Hermitage Landing, people alongside the road kept calling out to him, "Hurrah for Old Hickory"(he had earned this nickname for toughness and endurance during various military campaigns, especially the one to Natchez during the War of 1812), "Hail to the Chief," and "The People's President."This last title held a great promise. The first six Presidents had been a part of what commonly came to be called "The Eastern Establishment." Four of the six (Washington, Jefferson, Madison, and Monroe) came from Virginia, and were commonly referred to as "The Virginia Dynasty."The two Adamses, John and his son, John Quincy Adams, came from Massachusetts, so it seemed that the eastern seaboard dominated the office of president. Jackson became the first person elected in the "West," that is west of the Appalachian Mountains. Though not a "common man" himself (no common man could ever have owned a place like the Hermitage), he symbolized the ordinary citizen: honesty, straight shooting and marksmanship, down to earth, practical ideas and policies; nothing fancy, just the bare essentials of life were what both Jackson and the people who identified with him treasured.

Andrew Jackson was many things—lawyer, judge, congressman, senator, governor of Florida, store operator, race horse expert, duelist, fist-fighter—but most Americans remembered him as the victor of two major battles in the War of 1812: Horseshoe Bend in Alabama territory primarily against Creek Indians and the Battle of New Orleans in January 1815, where he bested the British. His opponents suffered grievous losses; his army very few. After New Orleans, people of political standing started talking seriously about running him for President.

He did run in 1824, but since no one received an electoral majority in the voting, the election went to the House of Representatives.

There, orchestrated, some said, by Henry Clay of Kentucky, the vote went to John Quincy Adams, son of the first vice-president of the United States and the second president. Jackson and his forces began campaigning as early as 1825 for the next election, which would be in 1828. More people voted in 1828 than ever before in the country's history. For example, in 1824, less than half a million people took part in the U.S. presidential election. In 1828, some 1,250,000 citizens "exercised the franchise," by taking advantage of their right to vote; in effect, creating a political revolution. Most of them voted for Andrew Jackson.

The reason so many people voted came about because property requirements for political purposes had been rescinded in one state after another; there was a time when an individual had to have so much money to run for office, and so much to vote. Now, some newly-admitted states (and some old ones, too) created white, manhood suffrage. This meant that if one were a man and white and over 21 years of age, he could vote. These combinations of forces put Andrew Jackson into the Executive Mansion (during Theodore Roosevelt's tenure as President in the early 20th century, the place's name was changed officially to the White House).

Rachel, Andrew's wife, was the person he loved most in the world. She was described by one writer as "gay, bold and handsome, with raven hair, splendid figure, and dimples."[1] Nothing pleased the couple more than to sit in the living room of the Hermitage, in front of a blazing fire from the room's big fireplace and talk to one another, while both Rachel and Andrew smoked their pipes filled with tobacco grown on the grounds of the plantation. The conversations centered generally around economic and social affairs having to do with the Hermitage; occasionally, their interests turned to local and state politics.

Rachel had been wed before she met Andrew, to Lewis Robards, and it was not a happy marriage. She and her first husband divorced, or so she and Andrew thought. (Robards had applied for a divorce in Harrodsburg, Kentucky-still a part of Virginia at that time-to the State Legislature in Richmond. The decree that he thought was a divorce turned out to be only permission for him to seek a divorce). Rachel and Andrew claimed to have married each other in August, 1791, in Natchez, Mississippi, though no records of this ceremony have ever been found. The divorce, however, was not made final until 1793; the couple married in January, 1794, in Nashville, Tennessee.[2]

Andrew's enemies, however (of whom he had plenty) taunted them, saying that Andrew had wed a married woman. Furthermore, they implied that Rachel knew the facts before she took Andrew as her husband. The talk about Rachel occurred mostly behind her back because everyone knew that the best way to engage Andrew Jackson in a duel was to insult his beloved Rachel. One criticized Rachel at his peril.

In 1828 Rachel would have been most happy never again to set foot off the Hermitage. She knew this was probably not going to be the case; she had dutifully followed Andrew to Washington when he was a Congressman and later in the Senate. She did not like the city—it was low and swampy, and caused health problems. Besides, she did not care for the backbiting world of politicians.

When Andrew was elected as President on Tuesday, November 3, 1828, she began planning another trip. "Well, for Mr. Jackson's sake," she said, "I am glad; for my own part, I never wished it."[3] Soon after, she told a friend, "I assure you that I would rather be a Doorkeeper in the house of my God, than to live in that palace of Washington."[4] She mentioned that she and Andrew had been married to each other for nearly 40 years, and there had never been an "unkind word" passed between the two of them. Their only disagreements had to do with his public appointments, including the last one—that of being elected as President of the United States.[5] But, being the good wife she was, she knew that wherever Andrew traveled, so would she, if he asked her to.

"I could have spent at the Hermitage the remnant of my days in peace," she told her friend, Louise Moreau Davezac de Lassy Livingston. She would, however, have been "unhappy by being so far from the General… [and] since it has pleased a grateful people once more to call him to their service, and …he will obey…," she felt it her duty "to try to forget, at least for a time all the endearments of home and prepare to live where it has pleased heaven to fix our destiny." In this same letter to Livingston, Rachel ordered two dresses to be forwarded on to the Capital City, for her use in the festivities that Jackson's Inauguration would produce.[6]

Since several possible routes for the journey existed, it seems that she thought the route through Knoxville into Virginia would be the most fruitful. One suggestion had the couple go by way of Staunton and Abingdon, in Virginia, then leave the Valley and cross the Blue Ridge Mountains at Rockfish Gap. They would go by coach, and even some of the way by horseback, so the citizens could get a glimpse and possibly shake hands with their new President, "The People's President." A grand gala was planned in nearby Nashville for December 23rd, to celebrate the "native son's" ascendancy, with some celebrants coming from as far away as the Waxhaws in the Carolinas, the place of Jackson's birth, and staying at the Nashville Inn.[7] This was going to be a triumphal trip; confident that Andrew would serve two terms, Rachel contemplated her role as First Lady for the next eight years in Washington City. Whatever the route finally taken, Rachel and Andrew had already set Christmas Eve, 1828, as their departure date from the Hermitage.

One day in mid-December, Rachel traveled to Nashville to buy new clothes for the upcoming inauguration (March 4, 1829) and for the inevitable social events. While waiting to be fitted for a dress, she happened to pick up and read a pamphlet that some of Andrew's opponents had written during the late presidential campaign.[8] It was slanderous, making the most out of the fact that Andrew and Rachel had married each other twice and that Andrew had "stolen" another man's wife. No matter that these events had occurred more than thirty years before; it was campaign fodder, and Andrew's enemies made the most of it. She went home in a sorrowful and agitated mood.

On Wednesday, December 17, 1828, Rachel had an attack of what was thought to be angina pectoris, a painful condition that was sometimes called "spasms of the heart," with strong feelings of suffocation. She had complained before of "uneasy feelings about the heart," but they had passed on without any undue difficulties.

Rachel was at home at the Hermitage, while Andrew was out checking the fields. Hannah, her cook and general housekeeper, called her into the kitchen to give an opinion of the meal she was cooking. On her way back to her sitting room Rachel screamed, clutching her breast and struggling for breath. She fell into a chair and then forward as Hannah rushed to her side.[9] One of the house slaves raced toward the fields to summon Andrew Jackson. Dr. Henry Lee Heiskel was the first physician to arrive, followed shortly by Dr. Samuel Hogg, of Nashville.

Heiskel reported later that when he arrived at the Hermitage, Rachel suffered from "spasmodic affections" of the chest and left shoulder.[10] She had been bled before he arrived "without any manifest abatement of the symptoms." Heiskel and Hogg bled her again, and "produced great relief with an entire subsidence of all the alarming symptoms."[11]

Rachel improved over the next three days. She was cheerful, could sit up, and converse to some extent with Andrew, the servants, and friends who had come to the Hermitage just as soon as they heard of her ailments. Thursday and Friday of that week she continued to rally. On Saturday night, December 20th, however, she sat up "too long" and caught a mild cold, with a "slight symptom of pleurisy."[12] These problems "yielded to the proper remedies" (probably bleeding) especially those that induced heavy perspiration. To the physicians, everything seemed to point to a "favorable outcome, so favorable that they retired to an adjoining room to get some rest; as did her husband, who had not left her bedside for sixty hours, but Rachel admonished him in her weak voice that he must remember that the good citizens of Nashville were planning a grand gala for him on the 23rd, and he must be properly rested.[13] Rachel felt so well that she got up and walked over to the fireplace, where a blazing fire warmed up the cold December night.

Over the weekend of December 20-21, it appeared that Rachel was making a full recovery. On Monday, the 22nd, Andrew went to bed at 9 p.m. still anticipating the great party in his honor at Nashville the following night. The fire blazed warm and comfortable, and while household slaves changed the linens on her bed, Rachel sat in a chair with Hannah, who supported her, and planned to take her back to the bedstead as soon as the rearrangements were completed.

All of a sudden, Rachel screamed in agony. Andrew had just

removed his coat in the adjoining room when he heard her. He rushed to her side, finding Rachel's head fallen on Hannah's shoulders.[14]

He quickly embraced Rachel, and called for the immediate services of the two physicians, demanded new tests, new restorations, whatever they might be. "Bleed her!" he ordered the two medical men. They did. No blood flowed from her arm. "Try the temple, doctor!" Andrew desperately said. The doctor did, and only two drops stained her cap. "No more drops followed as any signs of life became ever more remote." Andrew commanded that the table Rachel was to be laid on, be covered with four blankets. "If she comes to, she will lie so hard upon the table," he plaintively entreated.[15]

The President-elect finally reconciled himself to the fact that his beloved Rachel was gone. They had been married to each other for 34 years; since each was 27 at the time of their marriage, this meant that Rachel was 61 years old, the same as Andrew.

He stayed by her side all through the long, wearisome night, most of the time holding his face in his hands, and grieving inconsolably. The vast majority of the rest of the country had no idea of the emotional turmoils their newly-elected president was suffering.

Riders were sent posthaste from the Hermitage to Nashville, to tell the Jackson Party Committee of this calamity. The Committee immediately canceled its plans for the big celebration that was to have occurred throughout the city. "The table was well nigh spread," one newspaper reported, "at which all was expected to be hilarity and joy.... Suddenly the scene is changed; congratulations are turned into expressions of condolence, tears are substituted for smiles, and sincere and general mourning pervades all the community."[16] All the buntings and flags came down and black drapery put in their place. The Committee issued a formal statement:

"Respect for the memory of the deceased, and sincere condolence with him on whom this providential affliction has fallen, forbid the manifestations of public regard intended for this day."

The Committee resolved that "it be respectfully recommended to their fellow-citizens of Nashville, in evidence of this feeling, to refrain from the ordinary pursuits of life."[17] Nashville's Mayor, Dr. Felix Robertson, and the city's Board of Aldermen, passed a similar resolution: [T]he inhabitants of Nashville are respectfully invited to abstain from their ordinary business on tomorrow, as a mark of respect for the memory of Mrs. Jackson, and that the church bells be tolled from 1 until 2 o'clock—being the hour of her funeral."[18]

Thus Nashville went into mourning; not only did the governments close during the hours of her funeral, so did most of the businesses in the city. (A week after the funeral, the Mayor and Board of Aldermen in Knoxville, "commanded" the Reverend Thomas H. Nelson of the First Presbyterian Church, to preach a "suitable sermon," in honor of Rachel Jackson. He complied with their wishes).[19]

Of course the Hermitage filled up with friends, relatives, and even strangers, many bringing food, all trying in vain to say a word or two that might comfort Andrew, who went into seclusion with the company of a few of his closest friends. The road between the Hermitage and Nashville became jam-packed with buggies, wagons, and pedestrians. Almost every public vehicle in Nashville was transporting people up the road to the Hermitage.

Some field hands broke open a bale of cotton and spread the white stuff all over the grounds at the back of the house. Christmas Eve, December 24, 1828, the very day Rachel and Andrew had planned to leave Tennessee for Washington City, was cold, damp, with a threat of rain or even a bit of sleet. The cotton provided a dry, steady area away from slippery mud. Those same field hands earlier in the day had tearfully dug the grave that was to hold the remains of "Mother Rachel."

The sad ceremony started at 1 p.m. Andrew's slow tread to the grave side in the lower part of the Hermitage's garden, was kept steady by the strong arms of his close friends, General John Coffee and Major George Rutledge, both of whom had served with him in the War of 1812. His two comrades held onto his shoulders and waist and helped him get to this scene that Andrew still denied was even happening. One person stated that Andrew "aged twenty years in a night."[20] There was no "heart that did not ache, no eye that did not weep."[21] The near-by Nashville *Banner-Whig* said that "sincerely do we sympathize with our distinctive fellow citizen in this severe and trying affliction.... Just as he is about to feel the weight of [new] responsibilities and duties, he is deprived of domestic solace, which he had so long been accustomed to enjoy...."[22]

The congregation, composed of friends and family were actually in the back garden, but on the outer fringes, thousands of well-wishers from Nashville and other surrounding towns and villages, sang some songs, which included Rachel's favorite hymn, How Firm a Foundation:

"How firm a foundation, ye saints of the Lord, Is laid for your faith in his excellent Word! What more can he say than to you he hath said, To you who for refuge to Jesus have fled?"

Andrew knew that Rachel, being a pious woman,[23] had "flown to Jesus," but that did not ease his heartbreak. Surely, in his saddened mind, he must have remembered the time in New Orleans just after the big battle there, when he and Rachel danced happily to the fast-moving tune of "Possum up a Gum Tree:"

"Possum Up a Gum Tree, Raccoon on the Ground...."

But those times would not come again.

The Reverend William Hume opened the obsequies:

"The righteous shall be in everlasting remembrance...The death of this worthy lady is much deplored...by a large majority of the people of the United States of America. ...In acts of piety, as adoration, thanksgiving and praise she took delight. ...She was eyes to the blind, and feet to the lame and mother to the poor.... We cannot doubt that she now dwells in the mansions of glory in company with the ransomed of the Lord, singing the praises of that Savior whom she loved and served while a pilgrim on earth."[24]

Another speaker asserted that Rachel was beloved and honored by "high and low, white and black, bond and free, rich and poor,"[25] and love now at her funeral was so "unaffectedly expressed by a wail ... loud and long"[26] in grief for the loss.

A witness at the scene said, "I never pitied any person more in my life," than Andrew Jackson at that moment. Jackson "caught my hand and squeezed it three times," and kept saying "Philadelphia!" Perhaps this reference to the Pennsylvania city came from a widespread rumor that Andrew would leave the Hermitage directly for Philadelphia and would stay there until the electoral votes were counted on February 11, 1829, so that he would be sure to ride into Washington City as the duly elected President of the United States.[27]

This witness had "never seen before so much affliction among servants, on the death of a mistress."[28] Some "seemed completely stupefied by the event; others wrung their hands and shrieked aloud."[29] Hannah, Rachel's personal and beloved maid fainted and had to be carried off the premises.[30]

She said later that when "Old Mistus died, we lost a mistus and a mother, too; and more a mother than a mistus."[31]

The funeral ended at 2 p.m., and again household and field hands approached the dugout grave into which Rachel's coffin had just been lowered. As Andrew Jackson walked away, tearful hands began to pour dirt over this precious cavity. Andrew waved to the crowds that had gathered, and begged them "to weep no more,"[32] and mourn Rachel's loss in silence.

He did address those who had congregated for Rachel's funeral. In a breaking voice, he said to them:

"Friends and neighbors: I thank you for the honor you have done to the sainted one whose remains now repose in yonder grave. She is now in the bliss of Heaven, and I know that she can suffer here no more on earth.... I am left without her, to encounter the trials of life alone... For myself, I bow to God's will and go alone to the place of new and arduous duties.... I can forgive all who have wronged me, but will have fervently to pray that I may have grace to enable me to forget[33] any enemy who has ever maligned that blessed one who is now safe from all suffering and sorrow... whom they tried to put to shame for my sake."[34] The old general, however, could not hold back his own tears, telling his assembled friends that "I know 'tis unmanly but these tears were due to her virtues; she shed many for me."[35]

He walked back toward the Hermitage, still with Coffee and John Overton, and they put him into his room, where he stayed awake for the rest of the day and throughout the dreadful nights of Christmas Eve and Christmas Day, 1828. Some friends went in to see him at dawn; he had not slept, and neither had they. He asked plaintively, "What is there left for me now?" His friends convinced him that it would have been Rachel's wish that he travel to Washington and assume the powers of state. To serve "the people," was tantamount to honoring Rachel's life. He began seriously to ponder these statements, because he had a nation's problems to look after. One of his early biographers, James Parton, wrote that when Jackson left Rachel's grave, he was determined to "stand by the people of the United States," and run the government with a "single eye to their good. But woe to those who had slandered and killed that wife! These two feelings had no struggle for mastery in his… nature. In him, they were one and the same."[36]

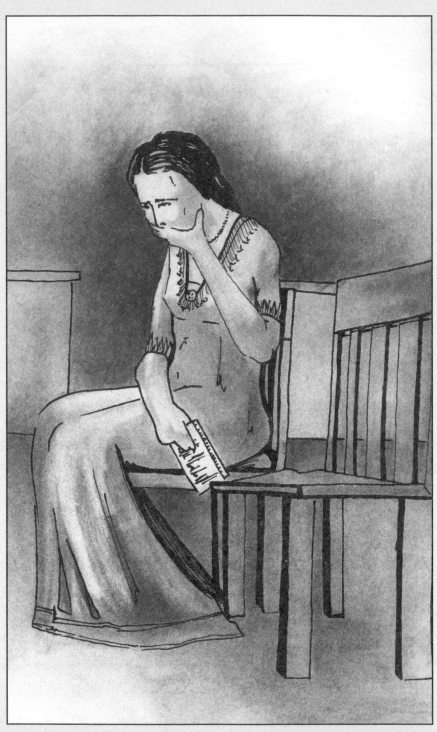

Mourning Rachel

Chapter 3

AN AFFLICTIVE DISPENSATION OF PROVIDENCE

As news spread throughout the state, region and, indeed, the country, of Rachel's death, speculation arose about Andrew Jackson's travel plans. Would he still take the route he and Rachel had plotted; that is through Knoxville, up the Virginia Valley, and across the mountain to Washington City? Or would the presidential party head almost due north through Scottsville and Bowling Green in Kentucky, on to Louisville, and from there take a steamboat on the Ohio River to Pittsburgh, Pennsylvania, and then travel by coach and horseback to the Capital? No matter which was ultimately decided, the overland route would be between 750-800 miles, taking at least thirty-two days to accomplish.

Primarily, the President-elect left it to his small coterie of friends and advisors to make the choice of travel, as they saw fit. The only condition Andrew Jackson put on the journey was that there be no fanfares or large gatherings of people along the way. This stipulation, of course, turned out to be impossible to enforce. He was the "People's President," and as soon as citizens learned which way he was most likely to travel, they quickly gathered by the roads and streams and way sides by the thousands to pay him homage. By January 3, 1829, however, Jackson had an inkling of which way he would go to Washington City. He wrote to Mrs. Katherine Duane Morgan, that "My journey to the Federal City will most probably carry me thro' your town [Washington, Pennsylvania]... I will call upon you... [and] manifest more forcibly than I can now [because of Rachel's death] the obligations due to you... for your kindness to my dear wife...."[1] Whether or not he ever actually visited Mrs. Morgan has not been documented.

Before any travel plans were decided, Jackson received numerous invitations to stop and speak to various political, civic, and social groups. The Pennsylvania legislature in Harrisburg, for example, speculated that the President-elect would pass through their city on his way to become the Chief Magistrate of the United States. Thus, they invited him to speak before them.

Andrew replied in a letter, probably written by his private secretary, Andrew Jackson Donelson (Rachel's nephew) that he was compelled to "decline the invitation…which under ordinary circumstances he would gladly accept," adding that he was "not insensible to your kindness."[2]

The Jackson Committee at Richmond, Virginia, surmising that Jackson might come through their city where the State Legislature was meeting, invited him to address the lawmakers. "I should be proud," Jackson replied, "to [pay] my respects in person to her [Virginia's] citizens." However, an "afflictive dispensation of Providence," he explained to the Virginians, had "deprived him of the solace of his life,"–he was in mourning for Rachel—and he could "not accept their invitation."[3] Moreover, both Harrisburg and Richmond were not located on the "direct route" that Jackson and his advisors ultimately determined.

Other towns and cities–Baltimore, for example–sent invitations to Jackson to visit them on his way to Washington City.[4] A "delegation of citizens in Knoxville, Tennessee, inspired Jackson to mention his "possible" way to the nation's capital. "So favorable an opportunity of manifesting my respect for the citizens of that place [Knoxville], and its vicinity, would certainly be embraced, did not the prospect of a steam-boat conveyance from Nashville to Wheeling on the Ohio render it probable that I shall take that route."[5]

He continued his message to the good citizens of Knoxville: "I pray you, Gentlemen, to be assured, that the obligation under which I am placed by your partiality and kindness, are much enhanced by the value which you have assigned to my future agency in the councils of the nation. The reward due to good intention is all that my humble abilities can ever hope to obtain… [T]he great interests of the country must be shared by the people themselves, and the faithful representatives… in the other branches of the government."[6]

Jackson's Party Committee at Louisville, Kentucky, wrote to him: "[We want] to express to you the earnest desire… to be afforded an occasion of presenting you, in person, their heartfelt salutations on your approaching tour to the seat of Government."[7] Speaking of Jackson's "exalted patriotism" in the service of his country, the invitation spoke of the recent election as a "proud demonstration of the incorruptible virtue and firmness of the people." His election, the Committee told him, would "serve as a beacon to direct generations yet to come...."[8]

In all likelihood, the most difficult invitation for him to decline came from the Central Jackson Committee of Kentucky, located in Frankfort. Several veterans, some of whom had been with him in his battles during the War of 1812, entreated him to stop by the Kentucky Capital on January 8th, and celebrate the anniversary of the Battle of New Orleans with them. "Were my heart susceptible of other emotions than those which a recent calamity [Rachel's death] has [caused], I should be very unwilling to forego the proud and peculiar satisfaction of exchanging salutations with my fellow citizens of Kentucky, and of participating in the celebrations of the 8th of January."[9] For himself, however, he lamented that "the present season is sacred to sorrow, and that which approaches [his Inauguration] must be devoted to duties."[10] Donelson, along with Jackson's long-time friend and neighbor at the Hermitage, William Lewis, continued to write regrets in what surely became the first "form" letter used by government officials in the history of the United States.

Washington City and the rest of the country buzzed with rumors about President-elect Jackson. When would he leave? Some said the 15th of January; others argued that it would be the 20th. Senator Daniel Webster of Massachusetts—no friend of Jackson—wrote that "General J. will be here abt. 15 Feb.—Nobody knows what he will do when he does come.... My opinion is that when he comes he will bring a breeze with him. Which way it will play, I cannot tell... My fear is stronger than my hope."[11] He also noted that "many letters are sent to him [Jackson]; he answers none of them." None of his friends in Washington City has "had any confidential communication from him."[12] Webster added that every person in the country seemed to be caught up in "Jacksonism," and that by his election they were being rescued "from some great danger."[13]

The Nashville *Banner-Whig*, in its January 3, 1829, edition, joined Webster in his speculations, and probably exaggerated the matter when it claimed that, "nearly a thousand stories have already been told about the intended movements of General Jackson." One version had it that he was going to the "extremity of the Union," to "traverse the snowy hills of New England," to avoid "the fatigue and inconvenience of a direct journey from his residence in Tennessee to Washington."[14] Another tale that made the rounds was of "steamboats chartered for his accommodation, and splendid carriages with snow-white horses, already on the way to meet and conduct him in pomp and state, to the palace at Washington."[15] The worked-up *Banner* writer had even heard that a "large detachment of Pennsylvania militia were to set out with their camp equipage, to meet their favorite candidate at the state line, and escort him with military honors to the Capital."[16] Of course, none of these scenarios worked out, or, for that matter, were even imagined. During all these speculations, Jackson sat quietly at the Hermitage, mourning the loss of Rachel; as a result, the *Banner* further reported that Jackson "had no idea of encouraging or countenancing any extraordinary or unusual parade on his account."[17] His only intention was to "proceed to Washington… in the most direct, plain and unostentatious manner," consistent with "comfort and hospitality" offered along the way.[18]

John Quincy Adams, the despondent outgoing President, definitely also identified with Webster's pessimistic view of Andrew Jackson… "Mr. Adams has no more favors to bestow," wrote Supreme Court Justice, Joseph Story, to his wife, "and he is now passed by with indifference by all the fair-weather friends."[19] President Adams did not have the warmest personality, and already had decided not to attend Andrew Jackson's Inaugural set for March 4, 1829. One story—certainly false—spread about Adams's coolness to all he met, dealt with the time Thomas Hart Benton of Missouri was almost run over by John Randolph of Virginia, speeding down the street and "blowing like a porpoise." Benton called after him: "What's the matter?" Randolph stopped long enough to gasp out to Benton: "Don't stop me now; I've just shaken hands with President Adams and my fingers are frost-bitten."[20]

All that most of Adams's, and now Jackson's, "fair-weather friends"—who did, of course want jobs in the new administration—knew between the middle of January and early February, 1829, was that their hero, Andrew Jackson, was on a boat somewhere between Nashville, Tennessee, and Pittsburgh, Pennsylvania, and was not easily contacted. He had plenty of time to think about his new Cabinet, soon to be formed, and other lesser appointments. His "friends" either tried to write letters to the President-elect while he was en route (and some of these letters caught up with him at big "stopping" points, such as Louisville, Cincinnati, or Wheeling), or planned to stay in the Capital until they could see him personally. When Jackson did arrive in Washington City, he had his hands full with people, many of whom simply wanted to wish "Old Hickory" well. But there were plenty of office-seekers with whom he had to contend.

Jackson and his friends finally decided that the most feasible way was by steamboat, just as far as they could make it on the Cumberland and Ohio Rivers. "He will go by water (in case the River, the Ohio, is sufficiently high and does not freeze over as far as Wheeling or Pittsburgh, where he will have a good turnpike (the Cumberland Road) the rest of the journey.[21] Should the rivers (Cumberland and Ohio) not be in "boating order," Jackson would revert to his and Rachel's plan of coach and horseback to Knoxville and then up the Virginia Valley, crossing the Blue Ridge Mountains at Rockfish Gap.

Most of the land routes, however, were unnecessary. He traveled from the Hermitage on the Cumberland, aboard the Steamboat Fairy, commanded by Captain Henry Harrison, to Smithland, Kentucky, where the Cumberland joins the Ohio. The Fairy took him upstream to Louisville, Kentucky, where he disembarked because a boat the size of the Fairy (eighty tons) could not get above the Falls. (It was not until a year later, 1830, that the Portland Canal was completed, so that sizeable boats could be "lifted" over the Falls).

Jackson then boarded the steamboat Pennsylvania, which transported him from Louisville to Cincinnati, Ohio, and on to Wheeling (which was a part of Virginia at that time), and finally to

Pittsburgh, Pennsylvania. In terms of mileage, the river journey of 1,128 miles from the Hermitage to Pittsburgh was farther than land miles. (It was sixteen river miles from the Hermitage to Nashville, on the Cumberland; 191 miles from Nashville to Smithland, Kentucky, where the Cumberland and Ohio meet; 316 miles from Smithland to Louisville on the Ohio; 134 miles to Cincinnati; 381 miles to Wheeling, and then ninety miles from Wheeling on up to Pittsburgh)[22] Once in Pittsburgh, he still had about 250 miles to go on the Cumberland Road (a part of the National Road) on into Washington City. This was a total of 1,378 river and land miles, nearly double the distance if he had traveled only by land.

Ironically, Andrew had decided early for the water route. On December 22, 1828, he wrote to an old friend, Richard Call, that "Mrs. J. was a few days past, suddenly and violently, attacked, with pains in her left shoulder and breast, and such the contraction of the heart, that suffocation was apprehended before the necessary aid could be afforded."[23] He went on to describe in this letter the close attention her physicians, Hogg and Heiskell, had given to her, and their optimistic assessments that she would recover. Andrew "trusted" that the medical men "will restore her to her usual health in due time to set out for Washington, so that I may reach there, by the middle of February...."[24] He indicated that the trip would start between January 10th and 15th, and if the Ohio stayed open in the wintry weather, he and his party would take it all the way to Pittsburgh. He added that "Mrs. J's situation will make this route necessary, as I am fearful that her strength would not be able to undergo the Journey overland, and I cannot leave her, believing as I do, that separating [sic] from her would destroy her...."[25] Jackson wrote this letter to Call on the afternoon of December 22, 1828. That night, as the midnight hour approached, Rachel Jackson died.

Although Rachel's condition was first and foremost in Andrew's mind for taking a water route, there were other reasons. First, he would be able to avoid crowds better by river than land. He deeply appreciated the care and concern of the American people; after all, they had put him into the highest office in the land at their disposal. But, mourning for Rachel was not compatible with fanfares, parades, and public appearances. Further, on a steamboat, he would have lodging accommodations twenty-four hours a day. If by land, he would have to leave his coach each day and seek lodgings. Of course, these could have been arranged beforehand, but with this unpredictable season of the year—it was middle and late January, and early February—the days were short; sometimes travelers had to stop in mid afternoon because going on to a further inn or hotel would have put their arrival well after nightfall.

The roads were sometimes not in good shape and, especially at night, coaches were vulnerable to mud holes, ditches, and other traffic. Moreover, at this time of year, snow, sleet, and ice were always possible. In these circumstances, the presidential party—like all other traveling groups—would have been hopelessly stranded. Although President-elect Jackson could have gotten a lot of help from his fellow citizens in such a situation, it was still not a sight to be contemplated.

By land, the President-elect would have been more or less at the mercy of whatever inn he stopped for his choices of food. Jackson, who was not in a good physical and psychological shape when he left the Hermitage, saw his gastrointestinal difficulties continue on his way to Washington City. At times, his system could tolerate only food and drink made from corn. He ate large quantities of boiled hominy, made from corn.[26] Another product that eased his stomach and digestive system was Kentucky bourbon whiskey. He usually drank a glass at lunch (generally called "dinner" at that time) and another glass at supper (called "dinner" today). His favorite was Oscar Pepper's of Versailles, Kentucky. Today, according to author Diane Heilenman, the Woodford Reserve distillery is a direct descendant of Andrew Jackson's favorite bourbon, Pepper.[27] Reportedly, he told one of his doctors that he would "give up" anything except his pipe, coffee, and bourbon.

Aboard the Fairy, and later on the Pennsylvania, food for the President-elect could sometimes be found in the areas through which the boats were traveling. Deer were generally available along the Cumberland and Ohio, and frequently hunting parties would spend a half-day or so-especially if their boats were loading wood-the fuel necessary to keep the steam engine in operation—

bringing in these prized possessions, from which fried and baked venison were made by the ships' cooks. Jackson favored all kinds of cheeses, particularly cheddar. Partridge, Kentucky hot browns, succotash, pancakes with milk, blackberries and Blanc Mange (French for "White Food," is a variant of a cornstarch custard with eggs and butter omitted), found their way to his plate, at least if his gastrointestinal system allowed them. His all-time favorite was spicy turkey hash, made preferably from the hens and toms shot along the way. Unfortunately, Jackson liked this dish better than the dish liked him, since it almost always gave him stomach cramps and a bad case of dyspepsia, commonly known today as "Indigestion."

In addition to getting the foods he liked on the rivers, Andrew Jackson's twenty-four-hour-a-day travel could be interrupted by fewer contingencies than by land. If Captain Harrison decided to travel through the night, he could send scouts ahead to see if any snags or shoals blocked the way. If they did, he would settle for the night. On numerous occasions he had to stop at "wooding stations" to take on the fuel necessary to keep his riverboat up and running. Even though the river route was much longer than land, he nevertheless made the trip faster by river than by land—about three weeks by river as opposed to nearly six weeks by an all-land route. All things considered, therefore, the President-elect made the correct decision of going to Washington City primarily by steamboat. He was the first President ever to do so.

In fact, Andrew Jackson was the first U.S. President since George Washington not to have had a direct tie to the government at the time he was elected (he had resigned his U.S. Senate seat earlier, in 1825, in anticipation of the presidential contest). He was most assuredly the first President-elect to travel such a long distance to take his Oath of Office as Head of State. George Washington left Mt. Vernon on April 16, 1789,[28] arriving in New York City on April 23rd, with plenty of time for rest and reflection before his inauguration as President on April 30, 1789. John Adams was Vice-President when he was elected to the highest office in the land, as was Thomas Jefferson (who also, as is well known, served as the first Secretary of State). James Madison, James Monroe, and

John Quincy Adams were Secretaries of State before they were elected to the presidency—all within close proximity to New York (where Washington took the oath of office) or to Philadelphia (where the government moved temporarily) or then, finally to Washington City (later Washington, D.C.), which was proclaimed as the nation's capital.

Jackson, of course, had a coterie of friends and advisors and their counsel in the matter of how he would travel to the Capital was of paramount importance. There turned out to be, however, a catch. The Jackson group wanted the new President to leave the Hermitage on January 18, 1829. The weather had been "kind" for this time of year; the Cumberland was clear as far as it would go (that is, to Smithland, Kentucky), and even the unpredictable Ohio seemed to be calm, especially considering wintry conditions. January 18th turned out to be one more date that had to be changed, for it fell on a Sunday, the Sabbath!

A rumor began to make its rounds among various clergymen, newspaper editors, and reporters that Jackson intended to leave the Hermitage on Sunday, January 18th (True). It was not long before this report caught the attention of the good reverend, Lyman Beecher, of Boston, Massachusetts. He wrote to his friend, the Reverend Ezra Stiles Ely, in Philadelphia, Pennsylvania, that Jackson was apparently tempted "to ride on the Sabbath, at a time when it might injure both us and him greatly."[29] Everyone in the nation, it seemed to Beecher, were willing to give Jackson a "candid trial" in his new-found position of President of the United States; therefore, he possessed a "fine opportunity and affection of all the friends of virtue…"by not traveling on the Sabbath."[30]

The Reverend Ely dutifully forwarded Beecher's letter to Andrew Jackson, and added a few remonstrances or warnings of his own. Ely was "strongly attached" to the President-elect, and thus felt comfortable addressing him on the matter of traveling on the Sabbath. Beecher's letter, said Ely, would allow Jackson to "learn the sentiments of many of the thousands of your friends, and of your countrymen who wish you the highest honour, usefulness, and happiness in your exalted station."[31] He called Beecher the "most distinguished divine at present living in Massachusetts, if not in New

England,"[32] and his word was not to be disputed because he believed Jackson could be dissuaded from traveling on a Sunday, "except in a case of mercy or necessity."[33] Ely told the President-elect that "if ascending a river in a boat, you would, of course, and with propriety, proceed in it; but when on land, if the stage of Monday would carry you in season to the place of destination, I feel confident that you would set an example of resting on the day previous."[34]

One of Jackson's fellow Tennesseans, Charles Coffin, a clergyman in Knoxville, and also the President of East Tennessee College (later the University of Tennessee), wrote that "a general effort" was being made "to rescue the Sabbath from profanations which have [lately] mournfully abounded."[35] He urged the next Chief Executive to refresh his knowledge of the seventeenth and eighteenth chapters of Jeremiah, in the Bible, so that he would know "how certainly the cause of God will afflict a sabbath breaking nation."[36] If, however, on the other hand, a nation "hallows" the sabbath—a day God "set apart for His own honour and the spiritual welfare of mankind, it shall remain for ever."[37]

It seemed apparently all right among these various clergymen for Jackson to travel on a Sabbath if he were aboard a steamboat, because one could not find places to "rest" as well as one could by traveling overland. Inns and hostels were apparently closer together on a landed route than on a river-borne trip. Anyway, on a river-boat, the President-elect could stay in his cabin all the day long, and not in any way indulge himself in "worldly" activities such as hunting, fishing, going to concerts, speeches, or horse-races, buying a dog, fighting off adoring crowds, or numerous other "venal" behaviors.

It proved no difficulty for Jackson to postpone his travel plans for at least one day. However, while he was in transit, another rumor started, that probably he did not even hear until he reached Washington City. It was widely spread around that the President-elect planned to "slip in" to the Capital in the early morning of Sunday, February 8th, well before the majority of city residents awoke from their night's slumber. Supposedly he planned his pre-dawn arrival to avoid fanfares such as parades, cannon salutes, large gatherings, or even official welcoming.[38]

One newspaper, the *Connecticut Mirror*, apparently willing to believe the worst in General Jackson, compared his supposed arrival to an event that occurred during the summer of 1828. President John Quincy Adams left Providence, Rhode Island, on a Sunday, on his way to Quincy, Massachusetts. It was afternoon, at least after "divine services" had passed, when he rode his horse for twelve miles for the same reason later attributed to Jackson for planning to "desecrate" the Sabbath: avoid fanfare, parades, and curiosity seekers.[39]

Mr. Adams was charged in numerous pulpits around the country with a "disregard to decency and good order, and with setting an example of the grossest profligacy."[40] Not only did President Adams violate perceived protocol regarding the Sabbath; it was his manner as well that was at fault. "[H]is dress and all the minutiae of his appearance, were exposed to the public in the most ridiculous and disgusting light."[41] The loudest critics of President Adams on the occasion, this worked-up New England editor self-righteously asserted, were those who had not "been previously charged with either bigotry or illiberality on religious subjects… "Where there is the same immorality in going to Washington to avoid parade" [Jackson?] "as there is getting out of Providence" [Adams?] "for the same purpose, is a question which is beyond our ability to decide."[42] And, so, this newspaper, like so many others throughout the country, reported the news and allowed the public to make a judgment of it; ready, as always, to pounce on any person who actually had a different opinion from their own.

Andrew Jackson never intended to arrive early on the morning of a Sabbath in Washington City; until the last moments of his travel plans, he did not even know exactly what day he would depart from the Hermitage on the Cumberland, near Nashville, let alone when he would approach the Capital City. Within two days of arriving at presidential quarters in the Capital, for reasons of some importance, he delayed any kind of triumphant entry himself. The "ruffles and flourishes" would occur, but not on the morning of Andrew Jackson's actual arrival in the Capital City.

Once Jackson and his party boarded the Steamboat Fairy, Captain Harrison ordered the vessel to steam out into the middle of the Cumberland River. Here he followed the routines of dozens of other river people; if going downstream, get your boat into the middle of the waterway, to use the current to help propel the boat and save precious supplies of wood. If going upstream, the captain and his pilot sought to stay as close to either side of the river as they possibly could, left or right depending on where snags and shoals were located. River travel was not the safest in the world at that time, so professional river men had to exercise great caution.

As the boat pulled away from the dock, Andrew Jackson came back out on the deck and once again waved to the multitudes who had come to see him off. As the Fairy began to make its way downstream, many people ran alongside the riverbank, hoping to get just one more glimpse of the next president of the United States. Nashville was sixteen miles to the West, and the Fairy chugged toward it as it began its fateful journey into history.

Farewell to the Hermitage

Chapter 4

ON THE RIVER

There was a striking resemblance between the rise of steam boating in the 19th century and the growth of automobile manufacturing and aviation in the 20th. In the first instance, Robert Fulton was convinced that steam was a good way to propel a boat—or even a ship—if all the components were as safe as possible and properly in place.

He had trouble convincing the public that he could do it. Building a steamboat in New York, his project was viewed "either with indifference or contempt, as a visionary scheme." His friends remained "civil" but "shy."[1] On the big day in 1806 "the signal was given and the boat [the Clermont, previously known as 'Hudson River Steamboat,'], moved a short distance and then stopped." There was a widespread "I told you so," attitude among the crowds that had gathered along the banks to witness this "historic" event of steam propelling a heavy boat upriver. After a few adjustments, Fulton had his boat moving again, and the Clermont continued on her way. The crowds were incredulous, "as the boat made its way from New York on the Hudson, through the Highlands, and on to Albany."[2] Even then, there were doubters; many "experts" in the crowds lining the riverbanks remarked that this time Fulton had been lucky: "We doubt that it could be done again."[3] There are, it seems, always the doubters.

One person who read the accounts of the Clermont and comments of the doubters was Andrew Jackson, notable citizen of Tennessee. He knew all about "doubters" and how almost instinctively to distrust them—or at least fault them for their pessimistic nature.

A century later, the Age of the Automobile arrived. Ordinary citizens were very much upset as they rode horses through a town, only to be disturbed by the backfiring or un-muffled sounds of an automobile. No wonder the phrase, "Get a hoss!" was heard so frequently at the turning points of the 19th and 20th centuries.[4]

Furthermore, many of these things could certainly be said about aviation in 1904 as it had been argued against steam-powered boats in 1806. Aviation—as well as automobiles—had been known theoretically for hundreds of years. The great Renaissance man Leonardo da Vinci had actually included diagrammatic drawings both of autos and airplanes in his diaries and other publications. It was not all that unusual, therefore, for the idea of a steamboat not supported by sails, but by huge propellers, either at the back (stern) or on the boat paddles on the sides. The former became known as "stern wheelers," and the latter as "side paddler," which meant, usually, one big paddle on one side of the ship, or as ship building-techniques advanced, on both sides. The paddles were almost always enclosed in wooden sheaths to protect them from snow, sleet, hail, ice storms, or rain, anyone of which could cause the apparatus to clog, thus stopping the boat.

With paddles on both sides of a boat, the captain or the second-in-command, the first mate, could speed it up or slow it down, just as the sternwheeler did. In addition, however, they could change directions at will. To turn right, put the "brakes" on the left paddle and "rev up" the right; and, of course, vice-versa for turning left. (In fact, there is a modern-day version of the side paddlers—lawn-mowing machine that is called a "zero turn," when one wishes to go around a tree, for example, just lock one side and retain the speed of the other. This is fairly much the way sidewheeler riverboats of the nineteenth century operated. They could get around limbs, twigs, entire trees, and other boats much more simply and quickly than the stern wheelers). Although stern-wheelers could not usually perform the frequent close-order procedures of a side-wheeler, they did have the advantage of requiring the efforts of only one engineer to operate the paddlewheel. Also, "having the wheel at the rear opened up much needed space on the main deck for other uses,"[5] especially for passengers.

The Fairy built at Cincinnati in 1827, the boat that President-elect Jackson boarded at Hermitage Landing on the early morning of January 19, 1829, was a sternwheeler. This was no great problem for Captain Harrison, because he traveled downstream in his eighty-ton vessel from the Hermitage to Nashville, and was still in the middle of the river, with the current—the swifter the better—doing the Fairy's work for it, on to Clarksville and Smithland. It was only at the latter place, Smithland, the site of the confluence of the Cumberland and the Ohio, that Harrison experienced any difficulties. While he went down the Cumberland, he had to go up the Ohio all the way from Smithland to Louisville, Kentucky.

Confluence of the Cumberland and Ohio Rivers at Smithland, Kentucky. The Cumberland is on the right, coming up from the South; the Ohio is on the left, heading North. Photo by the author.

From Smithland on the Ohio, toward Shawneetown, Evansville, Owensboro and Louisville, he had to hug the banks to avoid being impeded—or even pushed back—by the swiftly flowing center of the river. He was, therefore, more susceptible to obstructions, such as tree limbs, sandbars and rocks in his path, than if he could have traveled in the middle of the waterway.

From 1806 to 1830, the steamboat nearly extinguished the uses of keelboats for passenger and cargo services on America's inland waterways. The keel boats, or flatboats were especially excruciating for those crewmen moving them up-river, when they manually had to use poles and oars to keep their contraptions going; in this respect, the steamboat proved a godsend. Moreover, the steamboat could sometimes carry twice the cargo of a keelboat. The most notable goods of early river steamboats (which could be kept under cover, and therefore protected from the elements) included "sugar, molasses, coffee, whiskey, ironware, plows, furs, clothing, rice, broadcloth, china, cutlery... hides, meats, cotton, and tobacco."[6]

Likewise, these boats, as shown by the Fairy's manifest, also transported passengers. One of them on January 19, 1829, was the most famous citizen of the country at that time: Andrew Jackson, President-elect of the United States. He was traveling on the Cumberland River, one of the great streams in the length and breadth of the entire country.

The Cumberland starts in Letcher County Kentucky, and ends in Livingston County Kentucky, with a wide swath through Tennessee. It rises at the confluence of three large creeks, "Poor Fork," "Clover Fork" and "Martin's Fork." Thus, as one author put it, the Cumberland (almost 700 miles long, draining 18,000 square miles), "springs to life full blown."[7] Its general course is westward, "with occasional digressions to north and south."[8] Above Nashville (previously called French Lick) there were 325 navigable miles[9] for the increasingly large numbers of steamboats populating its currents. In only a few years after Fulton's famous voyage on the Hudson, nearly one hundred sternwheelers and side paddlers traveled regularly on the Cumberland, following cargo and passengers.[10]

There were, however, many twists and turns, especially above Nashville, where sometimes complete esses, or "horseshoes," forced vessels to "come back" the way they had "gone" in the first place. Of course, these natural diversions slowed deliveries and passengers to various towns and cities along the way. After Nashville, the Cumberland did not have so many "sinuous twistings." While this welcome condition might have sped up things a bit, there were the "rough shallows" to consider and prepare for, the most notorious of which was Harpeth Shoals. Even before he left the Hermitage, Captain Harrison, skipper of the "Fairy," was planning ahead for Harpeth.

As early as the 1690s a Frenchman named it "Riviere des Chauouanons (chah-won-ons). And then, to the chagrin of English, Scotch, and Irish settlers, some other Frenchmen referred to it as "Shauvanon." The Indians (mostly Shawnee) along the river's path called it "Warioto" (some form of warrior?) An Englishman, Dr. Thomas Walker, led a party of hunters across the Appalachian Mountains in 1748 from Virginia to what is now Kentucky. According to local folklore, he gave the name "Cumberland" to this river in honor of Prince William, Duke of Cumberland, who had been a "hero" in 1746 at the Battle of Culodden, in Scotland.

Regardless of how it got its name, the Cumberland became one of the most traveled water thoroughfares in the country. Of course, Andrew Jackson had traveled on it before 1829—many times, in fact. He had gone to Natchez by river, starting out on the Cumberland and finishing on the Mississippi. But he was not the President-elect on these prior excursions. The public may have espoused an interest in him as a congressman and senator and, most importantly, a military man. However, they certainly did not gather by the tens of thousands on the river banks and by the sides of the Cumberland Road to call out his name in honor and even reverence and to see this "Westerner" on his way to the Capital City. Jackson was the first President-elect ever to travel mostly by water on his way to his Inauguration. When Andrew Jackson took office on March 4, 1829, the age of the steamboat was in full swing; when he prepared to leave office in the mid 1830s, the era of the railroads was close at hand. On his trips back to the Hermitage while he was President, and on his return journeys to Washington City, he partially used the developing rail systems throughout the eastern parts of the United States.[11] But there was never before or after such a poignant trip as the one he took to his Inauguration in January and February, 1829.

Passengers on steamboats were housed on both decks. The upper deck was usually called the "hurricane,"[12] or "boiler" deck, and this is where most female passengers were housed, particularly on lengthy trips. Gentlemen's cabins were on the main deck "aloft the machinery,"[13] and usually just behind the funnel. President-

49

elect Jackson had such a room—the largest available—on board the Fairy, although it was in a fairly dangerous position. Steamboating in the early part of the 19th century ran the gamut of numerous hazards. In addition to shoals, snags, and tree limbs, boiler explosions were rare (about ten boats a year),[14] but they still occurred often enough to warrant the utmost vigilance against them. One advantage that Jackson's room gave him was that heat from the funnel tended to keep it warmer than the others, much to his pleasure in the middle of winter. Icing of the rivers at this time of year was one of the possible hazards, and Jackson, ill in both body and spirit, could use all the warmth his frail frame could get.

Several people traveled with the President-elect, many of them Rachel's kinfolk. Andrew Jackson Donelson, son of Samuel, was Rachel's nephew. Emily "Tennessee" Donelson, daughter of John (or "Johnny" Donelson), was Rachel's niece. These two first cousins had married each other, and now in Rachel's absence were on their way to serve "Uncle Andrew" in any way they could. Andrew Donelson would become the President's private secretary, while Emily served as White House hostess. They were placed in the same quarters on the Fairy. Major Henry Lee of Virginia, a veteran of the War of 1812, who had served with Jackson, was on board with his wife. Lee had strongly supported his old Commanding Officer in the presidential campaign of 1828; thus, he and his wife were invited to join the trip.

William Lewis had been Jackson's quartermaster during the War of 1812. In Washington he would become a part of the "Kitchen Cabinet," a group of informal advisers who constantly counseled the President on which actions he should take in reference to running the government. His room on the Fairy was close to Jackson's, so that the two could meet on a daily basis, where Lewis helped the new President, among other things, to write and re-write his Inaugural Address, and consider possible cabinet appointments and lesser assignments.

In the ladies' compartment—on the deck above the men's—was Miss Mary Eastin, another of Rachel's grand-nieces, and Mrs. Love and her daughter. Each of these persons had various and sundry jobs to perform for President Jackson, not only along the way but once the new government itself was formed.

In the lowest part of the steamboat was the "engine room," where the great furnaces were located; crewmen worked there day and night pushing wood into them, sometimes as many as fifty cords a day, to keep the boat running at top speed—somewhere around 10 to 12 miles an hour. An engine, or sometimes many of them, pumped water into the boilers that made the steam that moved the propellers. If the captain wanted to slow down, he could reduce the fire by opening the firedoors, or in some other way slowing down the draft. In these ways, and others, steamboating on the Cumberland and other rivers became, in effect, intricate works of engineering art.

The only settlement of consequence between the Hermitage and Nashville was Haysborough, named after one of Rachel's brothers-in-law. Her sister, Jane, had married Colonel Robert Hays and together they had put together a prosperous farm and horse ranch. Jackson's close friend, John Coffee, established a trading post in the area, and a general merchandise store. The Fairy reached Haysborough about an hour after it left the Hermitage.

Thousands of onlookers and well-wishers lined both sides of the Cumberland, practically all the way from the Hermitage to Nashville. As the Fairy paddled by Haysborough, the crowds cheered Andrew. He came out on deck, took off his hat and bowed low in a salute to "these good people."[15] He was bowing to them not as some monarch would to his subjects, but to his fellow citizens. These "fellow citizens" were overjoyed to have one of their own as an occupant of the Executive Mansion, or the White House as it was frequently called. The "Virginia Dynasty" and the "Eastern Establishment" had ruled long enough; it was now time for a "Westerner" to take the reins of government. Some individuals began to call Jackson the "Second Washington."[16]

Finally, at long last—or so it seemed, they got to Nashville, where another round of festive greetings took place. (Nashville was probably the fastest growing town in all of Tennessee: in 1804 its population was 400; in 1810 it had more than doubled to 1,100; in 1823, 3,653; and in 1830, less than a year after Jackson's historic visit, 5,566).[17] The Fairy pulled into the Nashville wharf, and at once a thousand or so of Jackson's fellow citizens descended on it to bid farewell to their new president.[18] Those gathered included Mayor Felix Robertson and the entire Board of Aldermen for the city of Nashville. On the Fairy's reaching the landing, cannon salutes were fired, with practically the entire population of Nashville on hand. Such enthusiasm for him caused Jackson to come ashore and shake hands with as many people as his health would allow. His spirits seemed "elastic," though it was still clear that he suffered a severe depression because of Rachel's absence.[19] His melancholia appeared now, as newspaper reporters frequently put it, a "silent sorrow."[20]

The Fairy did not stop in Nashville simply to let its citizens meet and greet the next president of the United States. The Fairy was a passenger vessel, in service for profit. Its main purpose in Nashville was to pick up several other paying passengers for the trip down-river, perhaps to Clarksville, Smithland, or even upriver to Louisville. No special privileges (except that he got the best and warmest cabin on the boat) were given to President-elect Jackson. Moreover, he paid his own way, because he did not wish to be beholden to any "special" interest group once he got into the White House. (This, however, was not true of most of his traveling companions, who gladly took the offer of a free ride from the Hermitage to Louisville, Kentucky). The cost of steamboat travel was quite inexpensive; one author put the rate at one cent per mile.[21] (In the early 1830s, railroads charged three cents a mile).[22] This meant that Jackson's passage from the Hermitage to Louisville cost him about $5.23 (It is some 523 miles from the Hermitage to Smithland on the Cumberland and then on up to Louisville on the Ohio), and extra for whatever food he ate which, in his precarious situation, was minimal. Some other authors, however, give different rates. For example, Byrd Douglas in *Steamboatin' on the Cumberland*, said that cabin passengers aboard steamboats paid $40.00 from New Orleans to Nashville, a distance that was comparable to Hermitage–Louisville.[23]

While Jackson stood on the Nashville wharf, with his right hand beginning to swell from so many handshakes, a large group of ladies gathered on the piazza of the City Hotel, overlooking the Cumberland River; they could see and hear everything that was happening below them. One lady exuded great joy in being kissed on the cheek by the President-elect; so enthused was she that she told everyone who could hear her that she would not wash her face for at least a month![24]

Unbelievably, a parrot in the crowd kept shouting "Hurrah for Jackson."[25] Many thought the parrot was a "plant," but, actually, Rachel had a parrot as a favorite pet (given to her during the time she was with Andrew when he was the governor of Florida territory). Her name was "Poll," and she was Rachel's favorite pet, so, of course, Old Hickory had a special place in his heart for her. One of his Hermitage custodians wrote to Jackson later that, "Poor Poll is doing well. She is as fat and saucy as ever. From her continued good health I think she will live to be an old bird."[26] (And so she did, right up until the time of Jackson's death in 1845. In fact, many of those attending Jackson's funeral were shocked when "Old Poll" let loose with a "torrent of profanity,"—which, in all likelihood, included Jackson's favorite "blasphemy," "By the Eternal"—necessitating her removal from the premises).[27]

Jackson heard at the landing in Nashville that a schooner, the Pacific, had picked up a live bald eagle in Key West, Florida, and was bringing it to Washington City by way of New York as a present to the new Chief Magistrate. Apparently this bird, the symbol of the United States, was received by Grinnel and Company in New York City and forwarded to President Jackson.[28] Whether or not he kept the bird is unknown; probably he did, for he was always fond of animals.

As the Fairy prepared for its onward journey, no passengers, including Andrew Jackson, were in their cabins. They were on deck shouting goodbyes to the people still on the wharf and on the banks, who continued their celebrations until many were silenced by hoarseness and even loss of voice. It had indeed been a loud, boisterous, and busy day in Nashville, Tennessee—and it wasn't even noon yet.

There were no timetables for the Fairy or, for that matter, any other steamboat plying America's waterways. The "rule" was "go as you please," but more practically, "go as you can," because of all the unforeseen causes of delay, such as trees, branches, shoals, etc., that might stand in the way of their journeys. Wood was another problem; if the wood were old and brittle it burned quickly, making a lot of smoke, and not taking the boats very far. Green wood generally made ample amounts of steam, and boat captains used it as much as they possibly could.

The Fairy slowly chugged its way out into the middle of the stream, caught the current, and plied its way down-river. The first major settlement along the way was named for the revolutionary military leader, General George Rogers Clark.

Stern wheel steamboat, circa 1829.

Chapter 5

FURTHER ON THE RIVER

All things considered, the cruise down the river from Nashville, Tennessee, toward Clarksville turned out to be enjoyable. The weather was fair and cool on Monday, January 19, 1829. (Morning temperatures had been below freezing, but reached the low 50s by mid afternoon, with a slight breeze coming from the southeast).[1] The center stream of the Cumberland flowed nicely due to recent rains, enabling Captain Harrison to cut back on the steam coming from his furnaces, saving large amounts of wood.

Shortly after noon, the capable chefs on board the Fairy announced "dinner" time. (In that period of history, "dinner" was the noonday meal, and "supper" was the evening meal.) The chefs and servers placed before their guests all sorts of culinary accomplishments: fried bacon and ham, cooked eggs mixed with oysters, beef steak, peaches—both raw and stewed—and salted fish with onions.[2]

It was a good thing that corn products were also on board, because Andrew Jackson would go sometimes for days unable to eat anything but hominy and corn cakes—frequently washed down by bourbon whiskey made from corn. His physical condition, made worse by his mourning for Rachel, greatly limited his intake of food and drink. He most frequently ate alone or had one of his close travel companions—generally William Lewis or his nephew Andrew Jackson Donelson—join him for both dinner and supper. On these occasions they often worked on Jackson's Inaugural speech to be delivered on March 4, 1829. In all of the early drafts, he insisted on saying that his greatest pride was in being elected by a free people.[3] This phrase, and his recognition of limited presidential powers, remained in the final drafts of his inaugural address. Besides working on his forthcoming speech, he also considered—briefly, at least while on the boat—the applications and nominations for federal appointments ranging from the cabinet down to local authorities. He received these letters at major stopping places (Louisville, Cincinnati, Wheeling, and Pittsburgh). He picked only a few of these applicants while on the way to Washington.

In addition to the passengers, the Fairy was also heavily laden in the hold with cargo for numerous down-river towns and cities on the Cumberland and up-river settlements on the Ohio. Included were large quantities of shot, powder, lead, rifles, satin, linen, gingham, cotton jeans, velvet, cambria, linsey, and flannel. Among the books were listed hymnals, Walker's dictionary, Cumberland almanacs and polyglot bibles.[4] Medicines also appeared in the cargo lists: quinine, asafoetida, laudanum, kreosote, paregoric, castor oil and epsom salts.[5]

Even with all its load, the boat could still travel at 10-15 miles per hour, an "unheard" speed for that day and time. In stormy weather, of course, the boats were slowed, but if the river was calm, as author John White explained:

"Passengers sat [on one deck or another] and read, watched the scenery go by and talked with friends, family and strangers. Ladies might knit or perform small sewing jobs to pass the time. The men might visit the bar for a mid-day pick me up or join in a game of cards. Gambling was a way to fill up the long hours of river travel."[6]

From this description, one can gather that riverboat travel in the early 19th century was a microcosm of American society itself with people from different classes and ethnic background coming together in a common experience. Of course, all the passengers on the Fairy wanted to meet and converse with their famous colleague but, on the whole, they honored his wish to be left alone.

Plenty of flora along the banks interested travelers on this particular trip, in addition to the presence of Andrew Jackson's cheering fellow citizens. A myriad of trees in their winter leaflessness lined both banks of the Cumberland. There were oak, beech, walnut, black gum, locust, redbud, maple, and dogwood, along with blackberry vines and various herbs.

Since the boat traveled in the middle of the river, sometimes it was quite a distance to either shore. Not being frightened, therefore, by the noise of the boat, animals frequently came out onto the banks and watched the humans pass. Sometimes, beavers and otters swam close to the Fairy, with more curiosity than fright. On the banks one often could see deer, wild turkeys, rabbits, squirrels, opossums and even a panther (commonly called a "painter") or two.[7] Occasionally, one of the crew members or a passenger would try his luck with fishing, and would bring in mussels and crawfish along with a regular catch. Perhaps the passengers saw a few Native Americans in their dugouts paddling close to the Fairy, hopefully to get a glimpse of the "Great Chief" on his way to Washington. When Jackson spoke to them—they were probably Shawnees—he referred to them as "children," and to himself as "father."

Despite all the good times on the Fairy, and developing friendships, there was one worrisome aspect of the trip that concerned everyone—at least those who knew about it—all the way from Captain Harrison to his first mate, down to the crew, and certainly to Andrew Jackson and his entourage, because they had faced it many times before. It existed about thirty-five miles below Nashville at a little town that is today known as Ashland City. It was Harpeth Shoals, and it ran about five miles along the Cumberland.

Though there were other shoals on the Cumberland, the Harpeth proved the most difficult and dangerous, composed of rocky ledges and gravel bars.[8] Author Byrd Douglas, in *Steamboatin' on the Cumberland*, remarks that among captains, pilots, mates, engineers, firemen and cooks, "every gravel in the Shoals stood for a 'cuss' word."[9] If a boat were caught on the Shoals, it would have to be "hogged" through, which meant that the entire crew, all able-bodied male passengers, and frequently scores of people from nearby settlements, had to get in the water—frequently in low water, not more than three feet deep—and "hog" the vessel through. This excruciating labor involved pulling and shoving by the men[10] while at the same time a boat's engines were revved up to such an extent that sometimes they caught fire, thus creating another major difficulty. If a boat could not be "hogged" through the shallow waters, its cargo and passengers were frequently transferred onto a smaller vessel, called a "lighter," to get through the barrier.[11]

At least one city profited from Harpeth Shoals: Clarksville. If the river was extraordinarily low, the heavier boats could not get to Nashville. Thus, Clarksville built up a "good river business" which, for two or three months every year, "equaled that of Nashville."[12]

Fortunately, none of the hardships that frequently visited steamboats deterred the Fairy on her way to Louisville with her famous passenger aboard. Many travelers considered that Jackson's presence kept the elements away and gave them good traveling weather and river conditions. Others remarked that the Fairy's good fortune was an omen of the positive things they believed would happen once Jackson got into the Executive Office.

One of the great advantages of steamboat travel was that in many, if not most cases, the boats could travel at night, thus making twice or more the time than over land. After supper the passengers on board the Fairy prepared for the night ahead, which could often lead to traumatic experiences. The boat almost always sold out all the available beds, sofas and chairs, for passengers to rest on during the sleeping hours. Not only on the Fairy, but on all boats on the waterways, rather strange circumstances and dialogues were commonplace. There were numerous "standees," and "talk they will, and a man might as well sleep on top of a piston rod as in the best berth of the boat."[13] An old man stuck his head out through the curtains, and requested more quiet. "Here, friend, lend me a corner of your blanket," shouted another passenger, looking for cover. "Here, neighbor," cried another, "I wish you'd stick your darn'd sharp elbow into somebody else's ribs besides mine." Another fervent request was "Shut your clam shells." "Turn that man's yoke," became a commonplace admonition to stop loud snoring. "I'd as lief fall asleep in a stew-pan," said one discomfited passenger. In fact, those with beds and cots frequently sold their prize places to out of sorts standees. Many brought along their pillows and a blanket and simply slept on the floor. Some of those who chose not to sleep, but to stay awake all night, frequently played a "wild and wooly" card game named "Shoemaker's Loo," much to the annoyance of fellow passengers who were trying to get a bit of sleep.[14]

The President-elect, exempt from all these "doings" himself, would put on his nightclothes, usually a gown that was the custom of the day. Before going to sleep each night he took a chain from around his neck and laid it gently on his night stand. At the end of the chain was an ivory painting of Rachel by Eliza Peale of Philadelphia, which Rachel had given to Andrew many years before as a present just as he was leaving on one of his military campaigns.[15] Her cameo was the last thing he saw at night on falling asleep and the first thing he saw in the morning, when arising. When he went into his residence in Washington City, he continued this practice, and also had a large painting of Rachel put up on the wall facing his bed; in the years ahead he also put this painting of Rachel into his bedroom at the Hermitage, so that the first image he saw at daybreak was his beloved Rachel.

As his boat plied its way to Clarksville and points north such as Smithland and Louisville, newspapers advertised artistic drawings and etchings of the General for sale to the public. Several newspapers offered "special opportunities" to their subscribers, at discounted prices. If a person bought four of them (for about $2.00 each) he could get a fifth one free. Newspapers around the country carried this advertisement: "The public are respectfully informed that the splendid copperplate engraved likeness of General Andrew Jackson is nearly completed. The artist, Mr. William Woodruff, has assured his publishers that correct impressions will be ready for subscribers this month," [March, 1829].[16] The plate was 12 by 14 inches square, and the impressions were "struck off on a superior quality of paper made expressly for the purpose." The Ohio committee (James Findlay, W. Piatt, Morgan Neville, Andrew Mack and William Burke), recommending this likeness of Andrew Jackson, felt it necessary to tell their public that each and every one of them personally knew or were acquainted with the President-elect,[17] presumably to let their readers and subscribers know that they were more interested in honoring Andrew Jackson for his accomplishments than making profit from his reputation and national standing.

The engraving of Andrew Jackson at the Battle of New Orleans, and its splendid denouement of 8 January, 1815, rendered by artist Robert Walsh, was recommended by various and sundry committees to the people of the United States because it showed Jackson's "stern integrity, long experience, and transcendent services to his country."[18] It was of a "noble charger" hurtling General Jackson toward the British at New Orleans, an obvious reference to the fact that Jackson's armies had suffered far fewer casualties than the British.

In February, 1829, while Jackson was still en route to Washington City, yet another advertisement appeared for an engraving of the General by a Philadelphia artist, Mr. Longacre. It was said to be in the "best style" of the new President's likeness, because it was copied from the latest portrait of Jackson by Tennessee's Ralph Earl.[19] "Competent judges," its advertisers claimed, attested that Longacre's etching was the most "correct likeness" of Andrew Jackson ever offered for sale to the American public.[20]

Jackson read very few of these "commercials" for his likeness to be spread around the country and sold in one form (painting) or another (etching). In fact, he probably slept when the Fairy passed through Clarksville during the night, although in previous times he had stayed there, primarily at the home of Judge James Elder, Clarksville's first mayor when it was incorporated in 1819. However, on this occasion, and with the acquiescence of Captain Harrison, he decided to steam right through the little city without stopping, although there were several citizens on the bank waiting to get a glimpse of him.

First of all, it was nighttime. Once the captain learned of river conditions (which constantly changed) he did not particularly want to pull into a wharf at, say 9 p.m., leave at 10, and learn that new conditions dominated his further trip downstream. For these circumstances, river men had created an elaborate system of communicating with one another, especially when there was some possible danger present. They had created "escape pipes," by throwing a greater than usual amount of steam into the air, which produced a loud noise and let other boats know your location. Up to this point in steam boating history, there were no whistles, or, for that matter, any effective horns. But there were bells—located generally on the "hurricane," or upper, deck. One loud tap of a bell to another boat meant, "go to the right"; two taps indicated "go left," three bells indicated that "I am landing, so stay away," and four meant "I want to speak with you." One tap on a boiler asked, "what is the depth of the water on the right;" two taps was a query about the left. With the Fairy coming down toward Clarksville in the middle of the river, and so many other boats heading to Nashville upstream, to say nothing of leisure craft wanting to see Andrew Jackson, traveling either to the left or the right banks, created a good reason for boats of all sizes and descriptions to stay in touch with each other.[21]

Another important concern for Jackson and his party about Clarksville was that he and the town's leadership did not, at this particular time, see "eye to eye" on several matters. Years before, on one of his military expeditions through Clarksville, he needed supplies—tents, shovels, axes, for example—but it seems that the local merchants, hearing of Jackson's needs, considerably raised up the prices for these commodities. Incensed at this action, Jackson sent his Quartermaster (probably William Lewis) to the merchants' places of business and had him requisition what he wanted and, under military guard, distribute these articles to the troops. He did give the merchants IOUs for what the regular prices would have been and apparently he did make restitution in the years ahead. But for years afterward, Clarksville was anti-Jackson.[22] There is no evidence on this occasion that the current mayor, James McClure, or any of the members of the Board of Aldermen even tried to call upon the President-elect.

One could attribute this official "snub" of Jackson to long-term memories of what it considered disrespect. Clarksville was an up and coming city, second only to Nashville at the time for trade and commerce; its importance belied any necessities for showing pique at the next president of the United States. Its major merchants in 1829 were hatters, silversmiths, wagon makers, wheelwrights, blacksmiths, carpenters and painters.[23] Laws made it a pretty strict town: washing (of clothes) in the river was forbidden, there was to be no work on the Sabbath (so maybe it was just as well that Andrew Jackson traveled through on a late Monday on into Tuesday) and no stripping and bathing in the Cumberland. Perhaps to console its citizens for all the taboos in town, Clarksville also sported three different taverns, which always seemed to enjoy very popular businesses.[24]

Just below Clarksville, the presidential party had now traveled some 150 miles from the Hermitage, so there were about sixty to go before coming to the end of the Cumberland. The first down-river settlements in the vicinity of Clarksville that the Fairy passed through in the dead of night included Gibsonburg, Spring Creek, Trice's Landing, Preachers Mills, Glenn Ellen and New Providence. Palmyra was the first sizeable town, along with Cumberland City and Dover, and on over to Kuttawa, "a picturesque little town… noted for its mineral springs."[25]

Eddyville was near by and "early on" it became one of "the busiest towns on the lower Cumberland,"[26] because of the output of nearby iron industries. (Today, many, if not most of these old towns have been greatly changed if not demolished altogether by the lakes in the area known today as the "Land Between the Lakes.")

All aboard knew that the first major stop for Captain Harrison and the Fairy was to be Smithland, Kentucky, at the confluence of the Cumberland and Ohio Rivers. Smithland, in Livingston County, served as a "wooding" station and since the boat was going to lose its downstream current, and go against the river up the Ohio, it stocks must be filled. If river conditions were especially bad, requiring either a left or right bank upward or perhaps either or both, a steam boat sometimes could easily go through fifty cords of wood a day, a devastating attack on America's forests at that time.

Besides, Andrew Jackson had kinfolk in Smithland, whom he had not seen since the days of the Revolution. He was, therefore, quite anxious to stop at Smithland's Gower House for several hours and renew old acquaintances and kinships.

Stern wheeler on the Cumberland, circa 1829.

Chapter 6
AULD LANG SYNE

It must have been a joyous, sad, and even tearful reunion on that chilly but fair January day in 1829; separated by war and distance, two branches of the same family came back together at least for a few hours. Back in 1765 in Carrickfergus, County Down, North Ireland, James Crawford and his wife Jennet ("Jane") emigrated to America. At the same time, his brother-in-law, Andrew Jackson, Sr., along with his wife, Elizabeth, and their two sons, Hugh and Robert, emigrated as well. James and Andrew had married sisters, Jane and Elizabeth Hutchinson.

They landed in the area of Charlestown (now Charleston) in the colony of South Carolina. Shortly after their arrival, Andrew Sr. injured himself while clearing out a forest for "new land," for future farming. He lingered a few days before dying in February, 1767, leaving Elizabeth, Hugh and Robert behind, with a third child about to be born.

Elizabeth did the only thing she knew to do: she made an arduous trip to the Waxhaws region between the boundary of South and North Carolina, where her sister, Jane Hutchinson Crawford and her husband, James lived. Jane and James took them in, and within a month, on March 15th, she gave birth to her third son.[1] She named him Andrew, Jr.

Andrew's early memories were of the Crawford household and the many children born to it, with whom he played as an infant and then as a young man. To pay for their rooms and board, Elizabeth worked as a housekeeper for Jane and James. Her sons, Hugh and Robert, grew very quickly, but she noticed in Andrew a love of reading, especially as he grew older, the Bible. Elizabeth kept hoping that by-and-by Andrew would become a minister of the gospel. Disturbingly, however, she noted a quick flash of temper when Andrew disagreed over some procedure in a game he was playing with his friends. But then the flash disappeared almost as soon as it occurred. Elizabeth prayed that in the future he would be able to counterbalance these two disparities,[2] one which illustrated politeness and learning and the other of temper and violence.

In the American Revolution (1775-1783), Elizabeth and her sons suffered greatly. Hugh, her oldest, at sixteen years, was killed at the Battle of Stono Ferry, southwest of Charlestown.[3] Both Robert and Andrew joined the South Carolina "Irregulars" (Andrew, 13, as a courier). A British officer ordered the two brothers, who had been captured, to shine his boots. When they refused he slashed both of them with his sword; the scar on Andrew's forehead stayed with him for the remainder of his life. (Andrew Jackson is the only President of the United States who has been a Prisoner of War. He is also the only President to serve in two different wars: the American Revolution and, later, the War of 1812). He and Robert contracted the dreaded disease of smallpox, to which Robert succumbed, leaving Andrew now as the only surviving child of Andrew and Elizabeth's family.

Elizabeth went to Charlestown to give medical treatment to American prisoners of war. She fell ill with typhus (some sources say "ship fever," from visiting sea-going vessels that had been turned into prisons) and passed away. Her death left Andrew at 15 an orphan. Knowing nothing else to do, he went back to the home of his aunt Jane and uncle Jim Crawford, where he stayed until his seventeenth birthday.[4]

In the early 1800s, many of the Crawford clan decided to leave the Waxhaws area of South Carolina and go west. (By this time, of course, Jackson had long ago departed for the West. Now at Nashville he was a lawyer, public prosecutor, judge, fist-fighter, and, according to some of his adversaries, a "scoundrel" and "ruffian").

The Crawfords wanted good farmland, as well as to escape the economic woes that seemed persistently to affect the Atlantic seaboard states (this was especially true when President Thomas Jefferson announced his embargo plans in 1807, stifling trade in regions from Boston to Charlestown).

John Crawford, son of James and Jane, was the first to travel. He came to Livingston County, Kentucky, with his wife, Martha, and, over the next several years, she bore him several children. By the appearance of the Crawfords in the Smithland area, a Jackson connection was clearly bonded. Andrew had traveled previously through the confluence of the Cumberland and the Ohio on numerous occasions, but apparently had not visited any of his far-flung cousins. He had always wanted to see them (some of the older ones he had seen; some of the younger ones he had not). Just a few years before his historic journey to become the seventh president, he had written to James H. Witherspoon of Lancaster, South Carolina, that "I have a great desire to revisit my native state, and once more mingle with those friends of my juvenile days who may still be living…."[5]

When word spread throughout the Cumberland-Ohio regions that Andrew Jackson was on his way, people, including his "long-lost" cousins, began gathering on the rivers' banks from Smithland, Kentucky, to Shawneetown, Illinois, twenty miles or so up the Ohio. (Some of his kinfolk had moved on up to the Illinois city). Many persons wanted to get at least a glimpse of the "hero," the man who was going to "set America straight" by eliminating undue "aristocratic" influences to empowering the "common man," thereby ensuring the rise of a democratic spirit.

Unfortunately, there are no written records of Jackson and his cousins meeting together at Smithland. The Fairy had to take on wood at Smithland, so Jackson could spend three or four of the morning hours in this little town, which later became the seat of Livingston County, Kentucky. (At the time Jackson visited, the county seat was Salem, Kentucky). Almost certainly one of his visitors was John Crawford, with whom he had frolicked as they grew up in "Crawford's Cabin," in the Waxhaws. John, like Andrew, was a veteran of the Revolution, having served with Colonel Francis Marion, the "Swamp Fox." One of John's sons was named Francis, likely after Francis Marion. Francis Crawford would undoubtedly have been among the Crawford branch of the family in Smithland to visit the future president on his stopover. One may safely assume that they talked about youthful days, their parents and grandparents, their experiences in the Revolution and the State of the Union, as well as predictions for its future. The Crawfords must have been comforted greatly by having one of their own on his way to the Executive Mansion (or White House, as some were already calling it) in Washington City.

The only certain fact about Jackson's stay in Smithland is that any and all meetings with the Crawfords or anyone else for that matter, took place in a large, respectable establishment known as Bell's Tavern[6] (later called the Gower House), which graciously made available a bed room in which the President-elect could rest, and also a suite where he could receive visitors. Altogether, Jackson's visit to Smithland proved to be one of the highlights of the Bell Tavern's (or "House," as it came to be called) history.

Built about 1780 (some accounts say 1800), it served as one of that era's "luxury inns," to accommodate travelers on both the Cumberland River from the South (Nashville and Clarksville) and the Ohio River (Louisville, Cincinnati, Wheeling, and Pittsburgh) to the North. Known as the Bell House or Tavern (its name when Jackson visited the place in 1829), it acquired its name from John Bell, who is said to have built it.[7]

Bell Tavern was located on Smithland's Water Street, named as such in 1809; later to be known as Front Street.[8] Since it was so close to the Cumberland, rainy weather usually flooded the front yard of the establishment. In extraordinarily wet weather, the basement of the house and the ground floor suffered frequent water damage. The house's walls were fifteen inches thick and made from slave-baked bricks.[9] Its two rows of windows on the front, facing the river, were of hand-poured glass and twelve strategically located fireplaces whose smoke went up five chimneys at each corner of the structure kept its visitors warm and cozy even in the most extreme weather.[10] Advertised as having twenty-six beds; one may assume, therefore, that it contained thirteen rooms for sleepy river guests passing through Smithland.

The person running the Tavern at the time of Jackson's visit was Stanley P. Gower, who apparently rented the place from Bell, who lived in Nashville. In the course of time, Gower either owned the place or became so identified with it, that the Inn-Restaurant became the name that Smithlanders dubbed it. In one of its back rooms, various court procedures were held for events and persons living in Livingston County, Kentucky. At the end of Water Street where "Bell Tavern," or "Gower House," as it was already being called, was a huge elm tree, known then and now as "Judge Elm." The first hanging in Kentucky was from this tree; later, several occurred on the lawn of the Gower House itself.[11]

Thus, it may be said that, well before Andrew Jackson visited this little town, it already had a substantial history. But beyond the place where he settled in for a few hours, the Gower House, what about Smithland itself, the community that had attracted so many of his kinfolks in past times? What would have happened to the history of our country if Andrew Jackson had decided at that time, or even earlier—or later—to go with them?

The Gower House in Smithland, where Jackson met some of his "long lost" cousins. The Gower House, unoccupied today, is one of two hotels still standing from Jackson's Inaugural Journey. Photo by the author.

Smithland (previously called Smith Town), was incorporated as a Kentucky town in 1809, and was completely and irrevocably associated with the two rivers, the Cumberland and the Ohio, that ran through its borders. It was, from the beginning, a community with a "wooding" station, which meant that restaurants and hotels sprang up near-by to provide for the hundreds, even thousands of transients who traveled through. When Jackson stopped by on his Inaugural Journey there were some 150 houses and 27 mercantile stores.[12] An English author, Christian Schultz, said that Smithland "appears to be the kind of [place] where runaway boys, vile young men and unemployed boatmen assemble," with gambling mechanisms that caused common boatmen to "lose their hard earned wages of a two month voyage."[13] There was even a pool table in one of the establishments, almost certainly Bell Tavern. In other words, Smithland was a wide open, gambling, river town that would take your earnings if it had a chance—or your life if it had to. No wonder, said some of Jackson's opponents, that he chose to stop in Smithland and visit his relatives,[14] since he was such a "ruffian" himself.

Smithland's future belied its 1829 conditions, becoming, as some historians called it, "a town that fell asleep on the riverbank."[15] Perhaps it relied too greatly on river trade, for that reliance caused the "city fathers" to decline offers from railroads, in the late 30s and early 40s, to pass through their little town. Nearby Paducah, Kentucky, gladly embraced the railroads and, as a result, expanded in many different directions, with a great variety of goods. To be sure, barges carrying merchandise and passengers continued through Smithland, but gradually the railroads stole their businesses.

Finally, Andrew Jackson and his party heard the loud bells sounding from the Fairy, meaning it was time to resume travel. After Jackson and his relatives bade each other hasty farewells, some assistants from the steamboat came into the sitting room of Bell Tavern to accompany him back to the boat. With Jackson now aboard, Captain Harrison gave the order for the boat to back out of its moorings, located just opposite Bell Tavern on the very narrow River Street, and to travel the remaining one hundred feet or so to the Ohio. Along the way between Smithland and Shawneetown, there was a little settlement in Illinois on Jackson's left, Rosiclare, and in Kentucky on Jackson's right, Birdsville, Bayou and Mulfordtown.

At the juncture of the Cumberland and the Ohio, Harrison heated up the boilers to increase the steam, steered the boat on a long right turn, and then headed for the left bank of the Ohio as quickly as he could. These maneuvers were quite understandable.

On the downstream of the Cumberland, the Fairy had used the middle current to travel faster down the river than would otherwise have been possible. Now, on the Ohio, the Fairy ran counter to the current; therefore, it was prudent to pick a bank, left or right, on which to travel. In this instance, Harrison chose the left, for their first stop was to be at Shawneetown, Illinois, some twenty miles up the river from Smithland. Jackson had other relatives there whom he hoped to be able to see, and besides, the Fairy needed the full complement of wood, which it did not get at Smithland.

Traveling on the left, however, presented unique problems. The chances of hitting sand and stone ridges in shallow water, limbs, or even whole trees themselves were ever present. In some instances, the Fairy, along with many other boats in the river systems, engaged the services of "snaggers," who went along the banks in front of boats and removed as many obstacles as they could.

Another huge problem for the Fairy and all its sister boats was acquiring sufficient amounts of wood, especially if they were traveling upstream against the current. One rick of wood measures four feet high, eight feet long, and two feet wide. It takes two ricks of wood to make a cord, and when one considers that some boats burned up to fifty cords a day, one can get an idea of how devastating to American forests these practices were.

Many times a steamboat, including the Fairy, finding itself low on wood, stopped along one bank or the other and sent out foraging parties to replenish their supplies. In this manner, farmer-steamboat feuds often started and lasted for lengthy periods of time. Quite often a farmer would see some of his cattle out of their fences; upon investigating he found that his fence posts had been uprooted and taken aboard a steamboat. Moreover, in some of the remote areas of large farms, it was not unusual for the owner to make a rare visit and find that great swaths of his timber had been felled, sawn up and hauled away. The most efficient woods for steam[16] boating were locust and oak.

Under ordinary circumstances, however, the steamboats would pull into a regular "wooding" station, operated by entrepreneurs along the banks. While the "professionals" loaded the wood, almost always stacking it in front of the furnaces to be thrown into the fire when engineers poured "new" water into the boilers—the ship's passengers frequently went ashore to explore their surroundings. They were called back to the boat by either gunshots or the loud ringing of bells.[17]

Another supply came from the wood towboats, which would line up behind a steamboat carrying passengers and merchandise and replenish its supplies without either vessel having to stop or even slow down. The tow boat would come up directly behind the steamer and lash its bow to the stern of the boat in front of it, sometimes getting so close that one could walk between the two; generally, however, there was usually a gap which on occasions led to serious, or sometimes fatal, accidents. The crew members from the towboat either carried loads of wood from one to the other, or threw pieces of firewood to their counterparts on the steamer. In this way the steamboat could receive a full supply of wood without having to stop. This procedure saved a great deal of time in travels both upstream and downstream.[18] By the 1840s in the United States, coal was used increasingly as a fuel for steam-propelled power. Unfortunately for the steamboat business, coal proved to be most useful for the newly developing networks of railroads around the country; but it may be asserted that perhaps coal saved a great portion of the American forests. Who knows what would have happened to our timberland if the river traffic of the 1820s and 1830s had continued unabatedly?[19]

The Fairy inched closer and closer to Shawneetown, once one of the best run cities in Illinois, before Chicago and Springfield came into prominence. The settlement was named properly because here, heading north along the left bank of the Ohio, Shawnee Indians developed this little community as what they hoped would be a permanent location. By 1829, the inhabitants of Shawneetown (still primarily Shawnee Indians) were not as upset by steamboat travel as they had been just two years before. One of the great attractions not only for Jackson and his party aboard the Fairy just before they arrived at Shawneetown was "Cave-in-the-Rock Island, featuring a large cave[20] where, apparently, ancient peoples had lived.

The steamboat Pennsylvania (the name sake of the one that would later take Andrew Jackson from Louisville to Pittsburgh) came through Shawneetown in 1827, on its way to New Orleans, and it caused a major sensation among the local populace. In the minds of several oldsters in Shawneetown, its arrival was a precursor to another earthquake. Many elderly Shawnees remembered all too well the great upheavals of 1811, just sixteen years earlier, and the number of tremors that followed. When the Pennsylvania approached Shawneetown, Illinois, "the people crowded the river shore, and in their alarm fell upon their knees, and prayed to be delivered from the muttering, roaring earthquake coming down the river,[21] its furnaces glowing like the open portals of the nether world."[22] Many fled to the hills "in utter dismay" at the "frightful" appearance of this "hitherto unknown monster" and the "dismal sounds" it emitted. Even lower on the Ohio River from Shawneetown, local residents reacted in horror, dismay and unfriendliness to these steam-driven behemoths.[23]

Misgivings about steamboats still existed, even two years after the traumatic appearance of the Pennsylvania in Shawneetown. The younger generation discerned that the Fairy, carrying the President-elect of the United States posed no threat to their personal security. So the "old people" stayed at home, and the "youngsters" noted this remarkable passage through their little town. A newspaper reported, "The President-elect passed this place early in the morning of Tuesday last [January 20th] in the steamboat Fairy, on his way, we presume, "[as though that were not already understood!] "to the seat of the federal government."[24]

At Shawneetown, Jackson disembarked for a brief time from the Fairy to speak with other of his cousins who had traveled above Smithland to greet him and, of course, he was always most anxious to meet those who had put him into the highest office of the land: The People! With a joyful heart, at least as much as he could conjure up, considering the gravity of his recent loss, the President-elect, buoyed by the wonderful appreciations of his work shown to him in Smithland and Shawneetown, made his way aboard the Fairy, on up to Louisville, where various obstacles awaited him.

Side paddler steamboat, circa 1829.

Chapter 7

ON TO THE NORTH

After fond farewells to his kinfolk in Smithland, Kentucky, and Shawneetown, Illinois, Andrew Jackson resumed his northward journey. It was 316 miles from Smithland on the Cumberland to Louisville on the Ohio, and the Fairy made good time even though it was now running up river. Temperatures were in the low to mid thirties (Fahrenheit), with skies slightly overcast, making it fairly easy to keep Jackson's room on the Fairy comfortable, with the warmth of the furnace and, in addition, the heat of coals from a brazier, a pan with lit charcoal that exuded heat—a way of keeping chills off since Roman times.[1]

In all likelihood, Jackson showed interest—since he was a farmer himself—in the numerous lands where the residents of Shawneetown had planted crops, primarily corn, along the bottoms of the Ohio River. A famous landmark of limestone, the "Cave in the Rock," easily observable from the river, caught President-elect Jackson and his traveling party's attention.[2] (Virtually all the way from the lower Cumberland up the river from Smithland was "limestone" country).

While not wishing to throw a damper on the passengers' and crew's enjoyments, he still reminded all of his party that they were not on a "holiday tour," but rather on a serious journey to the nation's capital city, where for the next several years, the course—and fate—of a country would be decided. Therefore, the decorum aboard the Fairy, even among the passengers, increasingly became one of sobriety and propriety, moods that definitely were not matched by people gathered along the banks of the Ohio to watch the Fairy pass.

Moving upriver, with the Illinois shoreline on the left, then Indiana's on the same side, and Kentucky's on the right, the boat steamed by little towns and villages, and by sizable settlements, their citizens on the banks cheering the boat passengers who (sometimes including Jackson himself) waved back. The Fairy made remarkable progress as it passed by Mount Vernon, Indiana (where the Wabash meets the Ohio), to Henderson, Kentucky, where the Ohio makes a slow turn to the North toward Evansville, Indiana. After Evansville it turns back gradually to the South and flows to Owensboro, in Kentucky. Picturesque log houses lined the riverbanks both in Indiana and Kentucky.[3] Even though he passed through many towns in the dead of night, hundreds of people still left their homes to await the passing of the Fairy. After Owensboro, the Fairy headed straightway for Louisville, through such little towns and cities as Rockport and Tell City, in Indiana, and Lewisport and Addison, in Kentucky.

With the passage going so smoothly, President-elect Jackson could devote much of his time preparing for the duties that lay ahead of him, such as adding to and deleting from an inaugural speech,[4] and appointments to cabinet and lower government positions. He could also reflect on numerous "hearsays" and rumors that kept spreading throughout the country about his intentions. Some amused him; others aggravated him. One of the latter surfaced before he left Nashville—that in his great sorrow for Rachel, he intended to resign his position as President-elect, perhaps even before he got to Washington City and simply turn over the reins of government to his upcoming Vice-President John C. Calhoun of South Carolina (who was also President John Quincy Adams's Vice-President). Nothing, of course, could have been further from the truth. It would have been an abomination, he believed, to the memory of his beloved wife, for him even remotely to consider for a moment relieving himself of his upcoming presidency. He had won the election of 1828, he believed, by the "partiality of the people, and that high station to which it has called me must be devoted to their happiness and good."[5] Rachel would have expected no less of her Andrew, and he vowed to keep this thought with him forever. He did.

Many of his opponents, however, latched on to the stories of resignation and played them for all they were worth, hoping they were true. They thought if Jackson should resign, the new president would be John C. Calhoun. At least Calhoun was educated—he held a degree from Yale College in New Haven, Connecticut—which was something Jackson couldn't claim. (It is true, however, that Jackson practiced law in North Carolina and Tennessee, and at one time served as a schoolteacher, so he was not completely devoid of educational accomplishments). As his journey got increasingly close to Washington, D.C., the rumors did not go away; in fact, they seemed to multiply.

In the meantime, Jackson and his party had to plan for their visit to the "Falls City," Louisville, Kentucky. No one, not even Jackson, knew exactly when the Fairy would arrive in Louisville, or how long he would stay or who would see him. His followers in the Kentucky city could make only basic plans for greeting the new president and offering him their hospitality.

When the Fairy was about twenty miles below Louisville, word spread in the city that Jackson was nigh. For his part, he showed fascination about the bottomlands he saw on both sides of the Ohio: they were about seven miles wide on the Indiana side (to the north) and some twenty on the Kentucky side (to the south). People from Louisville and surrounding towns literally stampeded the riverbanks on both sides to see the next Chief Executive. One such town was New Albany on the Indiana side, described in 1829 as a "flourishing city that makes a mighty fine appearance from the river."[6] The streets of Jeffersonville and Clarksville, also in Indiana, stood practically deserted, as most of their citizens were in Louisville, hoping to get a glimpse of Andrew Jackson.

As the boat came to the former ship building center at Shippensport, right at the edge of the area known as the "falls" of the Ohio River, its passengers knew their journey aboard the Fairy was at an end. The eighty-ton vessel could not negotiate the falls that raced down river toward it. All passengers had to get off the boat and walk two miles or so (more like three miles at the time) to the point above the falls, where another boat waited to transport the President-elect farther on upstream.

Work was underway at this time to construct a canal at Portland to permit boats, at least one at a time, one-way, no matter how heavy, to get through the falls, either north or south, without having to discharge loads or passengers.[7] Four locks were being constructed, each 225 feet across at the top and fifty at the bottom. Between 500 and 700 men worked on these locks and the Portland Canal. Work was "pushed" during warm weather and droughts; when it frosted, there was no work. A "beautiful" stone bridge held up by three arches and measuring 350 feet, spanned the canal where the turnpike crossed. The central arch was sixty feet and the others were forty feet, with the bridge's height at sixty-nine feet.[8] Piers on the canal were built of "ash-colored sandstone, brought from Knob Creek, Indiana, some nine miles below the Falls. The masonry work on these piers was described as a combination of "beauty and strength."[9]

Upriver, the Ohio passed Louisville West to East, and its streets ran parallel to the river. All the streets were paved with limestone, practical but "rough."[10] Jackson and his group did what was required of all passengers: get off the Fairy and walk a few miles to the top of the falls, and there board other ships. A constant "hack" service between Portland and Louisville existed for human passengers and "drays" operated to transport merchandise. On this occasion Jackson rode the hack part-way, with numerous instances of getting out to walk. Perhaps his "sea-legs" were getting to him. The walk was easier for regular travelers than for Jackson: admirers, all of whom wanted to shake his hand or, better yet, have a word or two with him, "mobbed" him. He was polite to one and all as he made his way up the ramps to the main part of the city, where supporters, belatedly, had made arrangements for his reception.[11]

Louisville's population at the time was between eight and ten thousand, with some 200 "good" brick houses. One of its highlights that always interested visitors was a summer house built in the top of a huge elm tree, in which twenty-four branches, representing each state of the American union at that time, was honored. An active theater in town kept residents and passers-through well entertained. Jackson was in no mood, however, to see the "octagonal" house (the one built in a tree) or enjoy a production of "Twelve O'Clock Precisely," "The Mowbrays," or "Two Mean Pieces."[12]

Instead, he moved—at least intermittently, because of so many citizens wanting personally to greet him—toward the hotel,

Perkins Union Hall, which the Louisville Jacksonian Committee had hastily arranged for him.

Located on Fifth and Main, the Perkins, previously known as "The Indian Queen," was often referred to as "one of Louisville's first inns to offer accommodations beyond bare necessities."[13] John Gwathney established it in 1803, one of many "taverns" and "beds and breakfasts" in Louisville set up just "as soon as the people ventured outside the forts"[14] (in which they had lived for protection against hostile Indian tribes). In 1819, the place had been refurbished and named Union Hall. One English traveler noted that each sleeping room "commonly contains from 4 to 8 bed-steads." It contained a "news-room," a "boot-room," with a bar (presumably for liquor), and a dining-room.[15] For dining privileges, the "first bell" rang at 7:30 a.m.; at 8, the "second bell" sounded, simultaneously with unlocking the door to the dining hall. The Englishman wrote somewhat incredulously that "the breakfast is consumed with a rapidity truly extraordinary; often before I had finished my first cup of tea...."[16]

Of course, the President-elect avoided all these procedures, rituals, and strictures. He arrived in Louisville on the afternoon of Thursday, January 22nd, still accompanied by the group with him from the Hermitage. "The General was received and entertained" in a "plain and hospitable manner, at Mr. Perkins' Union Hall, where apartments had been provided for him"[17] by the local leaders.

Of course, hordes of the Louisville citizenry, most just simply wanting to greet and perhaps converse for a few moments with the next President of the United States, visited him; some, most assuredly, searching for governmental appointments. Jackson met them all with a demeanor of grace and politeness, qualities that many of his opponents—and a few of his friends—did not even know he possessed. His hands had barely recuperated since Nashville, Smithland and Shawneetown, but they were certainly back in use for the thousands of handshakes in Louisville, Kentucky. One newspaper, the *Scioto Gazette* of Ohio, in considerable understatement, reported that, "during his [Jackson's] short stay in Louisville, he was visited by a large portion of...citizens."[18] Emily Donelson, Jackson's niece by marriage, echoed the *Gazette's* descriptions when she wrote to her mother that "I scarcely need tell you that we have been in one continual crowd since we started."[19]

He stayed in his suite—a parlor where he could meet visitors, a "den" for relaxation, a bedroom, and a private bathroom—at Perkins' Union Hall throughout the afternoon of the 22nd and into the morning of Friday, the 23rd. During this time, he frequently consulted with his traveling party: his old friend, John Overton, and, most particularly, with Andrew Jackson Donelson and his wife, Emily, along with William Lewis. Most importantly in his own mind remained the fact that he was willing to meet with and speak to common, ordinary citizens who were successful in making their ways through the crush of people to get to him. He did not limit himself simply to the officials of Louisville, or the "bigwigs" of the Jackson Party. He was, after all, going to be "The People's President," so he felt he should definitely comport with as many of them as he possibly could. Even so, thousands of Kentucky citizens were left out in the cold, simply unable, because of the huge numbers, to get in to talk with Andrew Jackson. He probably regretted that situation as much as they did.

Hotel employees brought Old Hickory his dinner, along with the prescribed glass of his favorite beverage (Pepper's bourbon from Kentucky) to drink, and other corn products for him to eat. He still suffered from gastrointestinal disorders and, unfortunately, had to keep a careful watch on his diet. Apparently, he slept well through the night at Perkins' Union Hall: his first full night on land since his departure from the Hermitage on January 19th, three days before. He awoke just before dawn the next day to continue stimulating political and social experiences.

On Friday, January 23, 1829, a warming trend in the weather was in progress,[20] which suited Old Hickory just fine, because continued cold weather caused the arthritis (called "rheumatism" back then) in his arms and legs to act up. He was far from being the only person in Louisville that morning up and alert. At sunrise, cannons began to boom throughout the Ohio River areas of Louisville and surrounding countryside. National salutes in the form of cannon firing took place at the landing where, later in the day, the President-elect would board the Pennsylvania to take him on up the river to Wheeling and then to Pittsburgh.[21]

The Pennsylvania, equipped with two large encased side wheels, commissioned by the Pittsburgh, Pennsylvania, Committee and commanded by Captain Kierstedt, sailed down the Ohio to Louisville specifically to pick up the President-elect of the United States. Unlike the Fairy, the trip on the Pennsylvania was free of charge for Old Hickory, and all of his traveling companions— paid for by the National Jackson Committee. This time, he took the largesse—he refused to do so with the Fairy to avoid being beholden in terms of debts to any specific interest; therefore, he had paid his own travel fare aboard the Fairy. He was, of course, given the most "luxurious" quarters on the Fairy, and certainly this practice continued aboard the Pennsylvania.

Numerous versions of the Pennsylvania had existed before the one on which General Jackson traveled. In fact, this was the third (a Pennsylvania had been built in 1818 at Philadelphia; another in 1822 in Beaver, Pennsylvania) river steamer by the name Pennsylvania. It was built in Pittsburgh in 1825 and was some 133 tons, as compared to the 80 or so tons of the Fairy. Thus, no matter the weather, the Pennsylvania was going to overcome river obstacles much more readily than the Fairy ever could. Surely, Jackson's trip from Louisville on to Cincinnati, Wheeling and Pittsburgh, was more comfortable than the one from the Hermitage to Louisville aboard the Fairy. (After the Pennsylvania that took Jackson to Pittsburgh, there were six more Pennsylvanias, one in 1832, another in 1835, followed by others with the same name in 1837, 1847, two by the same name in 1851, and one in 1854).[22] The average life of a steamboat was about five years, and the Pennsylvania that escorted Jackson to Pittsburgh in 1829 was lost a mere four years later, in 1833, on the Mississippi River.

Jackson walked again, this time the short distance from his hotel on Fifth and Main to the Fourth Street Landing in Louisville. Also, again, thousands of well-meaning Louisvillians came out at dawn to see Old Hickory and his entourage walk through the great noises of cannon boom, all in honor of the new Chief Magistrate. Not only did the cannon come from the streets and avenues, but from the Pennsylvania as well; many "shots" were ordered by Captain Kierstedt. Of course, there were no shells or destructive devices shot from these cannons; it was the noise they wanted and they usually got it. Sometimes a cannoneer would put wadded up paper into the cannon and shoot it out in tatters.

As Jackson got his first glimpse of the Pennsylvania he seemed both pleased and amused to see two huge brooms whose handles were made out of strong hickory, attached to the boat's bow, sticking several feet in front of the vessel, out over the water. In fact, on his way up to Louisville, he had already noted supporters on both banks of the river waving hickory brooms back and forth. He remarked that "they [the brooms] might be very useful,"[23] but just for what he wasn't sure. Upon asking further about the meaning and purpose of all the brooms, especially the ones adorning the helm of the Pennsylvania, he learned that the hickory brooms indicated that he was on his way to Washington City to sweep out the "Augean Stables."[24] Jackson knew what the phrase meant, for he had used it frequently himself; thus, he certainly did know about "cleaning up."

(The cleaning of the "Augean Stables" was one of Hercules' twelve labors in Greek mythology. King Augeas of Elis, owned several thousand heads of cattle and let them stay in his barns in bad weather and at night. The stables had not been cleaned out for thirty years. Hercules told Augeas that he, Hercules, could clean out these massive piles of manure in one day if Augeas would give him ten percent of all his cattle. Augeas readily agreed. Hercules found that the barns and stables were located between two rivers, the Alfias and the Pinious, so he diverted their waters into the stables, and cleaned them out in just a few hours. "Sweeping out" the Augean Stables came to mean any effort at bringing to an end graft and corruption so frequently imbedded in the world of politics. The intention of Jacksonian supporters in 1829 meant to show that the East had been in control of the country for so long that over the years it had resorted to scandalous and corrupt ways of running the government. Jackson was going to Washington, therefore, to "sweep out" the old order and herald a new one.)[25]

After being delayed by crowds pressing on him, Jackson and

his party boarded the Pennsylvania, with the Captain and crew out on deck to welcome them. The Pennsylvania swirled out into the middle of the river (the Ohio, at its widest here, was a mile and a half across from the Louisville pier). Numerous other riverboats joined the vessel, but one in particular was most fittingly named the Hercules and, like the Pennsylvania had large hickory brooms sticking out from its helm.

Crewmen lashed the two boats, using ropes (river men, however, always called them "lines") to fasten them together. Along the sides of both boats were railings which, supposedly at least, kept crews and passengers from falling overboard, especially in rough weather. Through these railings, end over end of ropes were threaded until finally a solid mass of rope held the two boats together. The Pennsylvania's side paddles were protected by heavily-encased wooden covers, to keep the Hercules from damaging any of its equipment.[26]

On board the Hercules was a committee of leaders from Louisville, as well as an orchestra playing patriotic tunes such as The Star Spangled Banner and Hail to the Chief on up the river, as the tied-together boats passed through little towns and hamlets such as Madison, Indiana, described by one traveler as having 250 well-built houses on a level bank with the river,[27] and by another as "one of the most pleasant and thriving towns in the State [Indiana].[28] Vevay, also called Nine Mile, settled in large part by grape-growing immigrants from Switzerland, were described by a traveler as "simple, amiable, and industrious,"[29] and Rising Sun, both in Indiana, and Carrollton, Ethridge, and Warsaw in Kentucky, lay in front of them.

All along both banks of the mighty Ohio, tens of thousands of spectators watched the Pennsylvania and the Hercules pass by their fair towns and villages. Jackson had ordered before leaving the Hermitage that there be no "public displays" on his behalf, an order that certainly was not obeyed. The celebrations seemed to become more joyous and louder at each place his boat stopped.

It was 134 river miles from Louisville to Cincinnati. After some 126 miles, the people of this Ohio city discovered that they were just about to be visited by the upcoming president of the

United States. The Cincinnati Committee hastily put together a delegation, and chartered a boat, the Robert Fulton, to meet the Pennsylvania as it bore its famous passenger farther on upriver. The Fulton met the Pennsylvania and the Hercules, tightly bound together. Very quickly, the Fulton joined them. Now, there were two ships fastened to the Pennsylvania, the Hercules on its right side and the Fulton on its left. Both side boats had political bigwigs aboard and orchestras which continued to play the songs of the day along with hymns and patriotic tunes.

It was a most impressive sight: Andrew Jackson standing on the forward deck of the Steamboat Pennsylvania happily waving to the crowds on the banks, the two boats, the Hercules and the Fulton, both tightly joined with the Pennsylvania, each of the three projecting large hickory brooms out over the Ohio River to show one and all that the "Augean stables" were definitely going to be "swept," with cannons booming both from the land and the boats. It was an incredible moment in the history of the United States as these three bound boats headed for the "Queen City of the West," Cincinnati, Ohio!

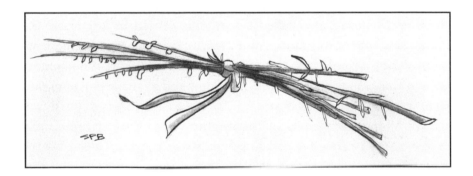

A ride through a snowy Pennsylvania countryside.

Chapter 8

CINCINNATI

Of all the speculations about Andrew Jackson's inaugural journey, none was more rampant than the question of what he would do to a certain newspaper editor, Charles Hammond, when he reached Cincinnati. Many people were much surprised that Jackson had not already dealt with him, in view of all the negative editorials Hammond had written about Jackson's public and private life, including Rachel. Other men had suffered consequences by insulting Jackson's beloved wife, and many now wondered how Hammond of the *Cincinnati Gazette* had escaped such repercussions.

One reason surely was that Hammond got into the business of "Andrew and Rachel Jackson baiting" quite late—actually not until the presidential campaign of 1828 was well underway. All the committees that supported Jackson had informed him to "bide his time," to stay out of any embroilments, not to be lured into acts of violence that might harm his bid for the presidency. He regretted very much, however, being put into a position where he could not defend Rachel against her detractors.

As Jackson neared Cincinnati, thousands of citizens surmised that he would get off the Pennsylvania, go over to the *Gazette* offices and at least administer a good horsewhipping to editor Hammond. Many in the crowds shouted out encouragements for him to do that very thing, and waved their hickory brooms in his support.

Hammond had a lengthy connection to Ohio law and journalism. He served as one of the first prosecuting attorneys in the Northwest territory.[1] When he began his work as the editor of the *Cincinnati Gazette* he received no pay for his first year, but thereafter, he was paid a thousand dollars annually. Also, it became fairly well known that Hammond received financial support, both privately and for the newspaper, from Henry Clay, Jackson's formidable enemy from Kentucky. With Clay's help, Hammond published a campaign newspaper during the 1828 campaign called *Truth's Advocate: A Monthly Anti-Jackson Expositor*, which was non-too-careful about the "truths" it purported to state. When Jackson was elected, despite all Hammond and Clay could do, the latter wrote a friend that the "president-elect has a path before him strewn with thorns [many of which, of course, Clay himself would lay down]. If he can carry the nation through all its present difficulties and his own, prosperously and safely, preserving the union, the Constitution and our liberties, I will acknowledge at the close of his career that I have done injustices to his temper and capacity. Meanwhile I shall be a 'looker on in Venice.'"[2]

Early in the campaign the *Gazette* published a list of Andrew Jackson's "wrongdoings."

He had declared martial law in New Orleans, , suppressed the liberties of the press and suspended the Writ of Habeas Corpus— all of which were just during the War of 1812! Later, as governor of Florida, he "exposed" the United States to war with Spain. In his private life, things got worse. He was implicated in the Burr Conspiracy,[3] he "murdered" Charles Dickinson,[4] and he "robbed Lewis Robards of his wife, in violation of the peace, the dignity, and the laws, of the states of Kentucky and Tennessee." The editor concluded, "In short, his [Jackson's] life has been one continual scene of quarreling, violence and bloodshed... Who, but men like him... can support a man of his character for President?"[5]

On a less libelous note, the "Clay Papers" throughout the United States, including the *Cincinnati Gazette*, began to argue that it was actually the British behind the efforts to elect Andrew Jackson as president (which would have been one of the great ironies of the day, in view of Jackson's life-long hatred of England). Under John Quincy Adams, the tariff (a tax on goods coming into the country) had become high; many people thought that Jackson would support lowering the tariff, though he did not make any explicit statements about it during the campaign. The British, according to this view, apparently thought that the tariff would be drastically reduced under his administration.[6]

A committee of Adams men met in mid-October, 1828 and, predictably, attacked Andrew Jackson, a meeting duly reported by Hammond and the *Gazette*. If General Jackson were to win, his policy would be a "progressive tyranny" and "usurpation" of rightful powers belonging to other branches of the government (which turned out to be at least half-way true). His policies toward foreign countries would be "war and conquest." There could be no "state of security" under a President like Jackson; if he were to be invested with power, it "would be just as rational as to bid warring elements to be still, or attempt to grasp a bolt of lightning in its course."[7] The committee "solemnly and fearlessly" appealed to the American public to determine whether "General Jackson possesses the qualifications" for office of the President, hinting that Jackson was ignorant of the workings of the Constitution, laws of the land, and the intricate details of foreign policies.[8]

The Clay newspapers, including the *Gazette*, did see their way from time to time to insert a bit of humor into their diatribes. One, *The New York Commercial*, made fun of an effort by a group of Jackson supporters to plant a hickory tree, "the emblem of Jackson idolatry," in front of Tammany Hall. After tearing up several "unoffending stones," the group was ordered to leave, saying that otherwise, they would be put in jail. They departed the scene.[9] Back in Ohio, the *Gazette* gleefully reported that in Washington City, the capital, "two-thousand dollars had been subscribed" to procure the "largest and nicest hickory tree that grows in Pennsylvania, taking it to Washington, and planting it in front of the President's house." A speech was to be made by a member of the Washington "Hickory Club": "Here's a nice old Hickory, for to please your Majesty." General Jackson, the *Gazette* surmised, would answer: "Oh Ye men of Hickoreee; Good Lord! What fools you be!"

But, as time passed, Hammond, the *Gazette*, and other Clay papers, seemed increasingly to personalize their attacks against Jackson, particularly relating to Rachel. Most understood that Jackson could withstand political criticism, but attacks on Rachel had always been something else, and this is what caused so many people to wonder why he didn't bring down Mr. Hammond. Some of Hammond's statements reflected his views (and, definitely those of Henry Clay and John Quincy Adams) that as the country's First

Lady she would be open to close scrutiny by the press and public opinion. "Ought a[n] adulteress and her paramour husband...be placed in the highest office?" "When they [Rachel and Andrew] assumed the open relation of husband and wife, it was an illegal and criminal act. They are the mere creatures of passion."[10]

Obviously, more people stood up for Jackson than those who supported the likes of Charles Hammond and his *Cincinnati Gazette*. Apparently, after Rachel's death, Hammond found other venues for his ranting. He began writing editorials against Mrs. Susan Decatur, wife of the Commodore, who had laid various claims before the U.S. Congress, for services rendered by her late husband. Speaking of the inactivity in this regard of both houses (though at one time her claims bill was passed by the Senate), Hammond let it be known that he thought she was non-deserving. This point of view angered many people, including the editors at the *Hagerstown* (Maryland) *Mail*, who sniffily reported that "the traducer and slanderer of Mrs. Jackson, has let loose the flood gates of his venom on Mrs. Decatur, the widow of the departed gallant Commodore Decatur, one of Columbus's bravest sons. To assail the characters or motives of virtuous females appears to be his peculiar prerogative."[11] This "dastard" must, the paper asserted, "vent his spleen upon someone—and he prudently chooses a defenseless woman. This is in perfect accordance with his character, so lately made manifest in assaults on the character of the lamented Mrs. Jackson."[12]

Whatever his negative assessments of Jackson were, the editor failed. Jackson was elected overwhelmingly to be the seventh President of the United States. And the people all the way from the Hermitage, through Clarksville, Tennessee; Smithland, Kentucky; Shawneetown, Illinois; and Louisville, Kentucky; let him know they supported him. And, this wonderful feeling of a western, and democratic, president-elect only buoyed up everyone's spirits along the way.

In Cincinnati, a Jackson supporter, Robert Punshon, wrote to the President-elect, and said, "It has long been contemplated that the public printing in this city will be removed from the present incumbent, C. Hammond of the *Gazette*."[13] A truer prediction was never made than this one; certainly, Jackson intended to change Cincinnati governmental publishers once he was securely in the White House. He did not go to the editorial offices of the *Gazette* (much to the disappointment of some of his followers), and Mr. Hammond did not come to see the President-elect, who spent his time in Cincinnati greeting those who warmly welcomed him.

Cincinnati in early 1829 was probably the most flourishing city in the West and was a "crossroads" of sorts between North and South, with large quantities of goods both arriving and departing from the city. One of its nicknames was "Porkopolis," because of all the meat products that passed through its import and export facilities. In 1819, Cincinnati's population was reported at 9,642[14]; a scant ten years later, its citizens numbered some 22,000[15] with an estimated $2.8 million in manufactured products.[16] Its chief exports were flour, pork, lard, whiskey and tobacco; its imports consisted mostly of salt, sugar, tea, dry goods iron products, lumber and cotton.[17]

Apparently, of all the business places in Cincinnati, none flourished more than taverns and "coffee houses," and, according to one source, it was sometimes quite difficult to tell the difference between the two.[18] In fact, right about the time Jackson passed through, a large local battle was brewing over the taxation of these establishments. Much of the city's populace wanted a drastic reduction, if not outright repeal, of licensing taxes for these concerns. *The Chronicle* opposed such measures, saying that "daily visitors" of these places were not overburdened with taxes of any sort. Besides, if the taxes were removed, the "number of these tippling houses will be prodigiously increased, and consequently the temptations to intemperance and vice proportionably multiplied."[19] Of course, the President-elect voiced no opinions on these matters, considering them to be purely local in nature.

A major concern of the presidential party passing through Cincinnati was that there had been sporadic smallpox outbreaks during most of the previous year. On January 31, 1829, just a few days after Jackson's visit, there were one hundred confirmed cases of the dreaded disease in the city.[20] Although Jackson had already suffered smallpox as a teen-age soldier in the Revolution, he and his fellow travelers nevertheless received inoculations while in Cincinnati. The smallpox vaccine was administered in 1829 the same way it is today, by pricking the skin with a virus-laden lancet or needle.

But it had not always been that way. The ancient Chinese used to take the scab from a dried up smallpox blister, grind it into a fine dust, and blow it up the nose of a healthy person. Even more bizarre, perhaps, was the work of an American colonist in the 1720s, Cotton Mather, who gave oral dosages—called variolation—of smallpox to a healthy person in the belief that it would cause a mild case of the malady, thus setting up an immunity to the real thing.[21] Like the Chinese, he achieved much success in his efforts to stem the spread of this miserable disease. Vaccination proved so practical that many years later, in the American Revolution, General George Washington had all his troops vaccinated for smallpox: by and large, these inoculations helped his troops to stay healthy. In late 18th century an Englishman, Dr. Edward Jenner of Gloucestershire created the vaccination process of piercing the skin; even for several years afterwards, however, the scab from the sore caused by the vaccination was taken off, dissolved in water and given to the "victim" to drink.[22] While certainly not unusual, therefore, for Jackson to take this smallpox preventative as he was en-route to Washington City, he and his group were spared the "scab-dissolved-in-water" method of administering the doses.

The Cincinnati that welcomed President-elect Jackson contained some engineering and technical marvels. As the Ohio flowed through Cincinnati, one could see the descending angles of stone-paved streets, enabling stagnant water and other waste materials to be washed away during heavy rains, into the river,[23] a clever bit of engineering, according to widely held opinion. The first bank away from the river was called "The Bottom," and the second bank, "The Hill."[24] A branch Bank of the United States was among its most notable buildings (two stories high with a front of sixty feet). There were numerous churches in the city, none of which featured any "remarkable architecture," the main theatre was "beggarly," and the Cincinnati College was "not much better."[25] Three market houses, each of which was three hundred feet long,[26] offered what was probably the best selection of foodstuff in the entire Western regions. The only place one traveler, John Sharkey, found to have any artistic value was the Appolonian Gardens,[27] created at Deer Park by some members of Cincinnati's large German population to foster a society for the arts (especially "lieder" or songs) and literature. Mrs. Frances Trollope, a visitor to Cincinnati from England, confirmed Sharkey's opinion of the city when she wrote that an "uninteresting mass of buildings created a "crude and noisy town."[28]

Trollope, not particularly an admirer of American life and customs, seemed to be taken in—as thousands of others were—by the patriotic fervor of Andrew Jackson's arrival in town. "The noble steam-boat," she admiringly wrote, was "flanked on each side by one [the Hercules and the Fulton] of nearly equal size and splendour [sic]; the roofs of all three were covered by a crowd of men; cannon saluted them from the shore as they passed by, to the distance of a quarter of a mile above the town; there they turned about and came back down the river with a rapid but stately union, the three vessels so close together as to appear one mighty mass upon the water."[29]

The three tightly-bound boats turned a sharp left and went over to the side of the river, near Covington, Kentucky. There, the crews hurriedly and accurately separated the vessels, untying and pulling the lines from the railings, so that only the Pennsylvania would make it to Cincinnati's main landing place, a wharf fronting the city. Mrs. Trollope was quite impressed: "All this maneuvering was extremely well executed, and really beautiful."[30]

While the Pennsylvania made its way across the river, with the Hercules and Fulton steaming close behind, and with many other river vessels of all sorts and descriptions following along, cannon salutes continued to split the air. From the shore, Captain Henry Tatem's artillery company fired off several cannons, while on the Pennsylvania, Captain Kierstedt answered in kind.[31] The music bands on both the boats on the river and in dock synchronized their efforts, in playing patriotic songs, with a continued emphasis on Hail to the Chief. The crews of two large vessels, the Caledonia and the Brandywine, joined in the cannonading, greeting the new Chief Executive of the United States.[32] A "mass of heads" waited on the Cincinnati wharf and surrounding areas; "crowds of ladies" waved their handkerchiefs, and the men "greeted the veteran hero with hearty cheers."[33]

Mrs. Trollope remarked on the "quietness" of the crowds, which waited on the shore "in perfect stillness."[34] The relative silence of the crowds did not reflect any feelings of hostility toward Jackson; indeed, during the recent campaign he had been "decidedly" the popular candidate in Cincinnati and surrounding areas.[35] Many, if not most, of the people in the crowds were showing respect for the President-elect, especially in view of Rachel's recent death. This, however, did not stop a few from shouting "Hurrah for Adams!" as the Pennsylvania neared the great Cincinnati wharf.

Numerous private carriages along the wharf competed to have the honor of taking Jackson to his headquarters at the Cincinnati Hotel. It was now about two in the afternoon of Saturday, January 24, 1829. The weather was fair, but cold—around 30 degrees—so, as at Louisville, Old Hickory decided to walk most of the distance; accordingly, the crowds divided themselves to give him enough room. He looked better than many had expected,[36] to the pleasure of most observers and the chagrin of a few. He and a "handful of European men" walked bareheaded in the crowd; his gray hair "was carelessly but not ungracefully arranged," and in spite of his "gaunt features," he looked "like a gentleman and a soldier."[37]

As Jackson made his way through the crowds, one obvious Adams-Clay man shouted out, "Adams forever!" and another remarked, "There goes Jackson; where is his wife?"[38] The man spoke these words either from ignorance of Rachel's death, or an effort to nettle Jackson over her divorce proceedings, so many years before. The President-elect kept walking until he came to the Cincinnati Hotel, where he spent most of the remainder of the afternoon. The local committee had hastily set up a suite of rooms, primarily to afford privacy and rest. Nevertheless, he was "almost incessantly occupied in taking by the hand the crowds of both sexes, and of all ages who waited on him," and "spoke to them with that easy politeness and affability for which he is peculiarly distinguished."[39]

While the President-elect was trying to get some rest and comfort at the Cincinnati Hotel, the group traveling with him had to make some determinations about the remaining segments of their journey. One of the reasons why they stopped at Cincinnati was to give Donelson and Lewis and their traveling companions an opportunity to study weather and river conditions, and hopefully to make some enlightened predictions about them. Besides, the Pennsylvania needed to spend a few hours re-supplying wood and taking on water for steam. When these deliberations had been in progress for several hours, Jackson left the Cincinnati Hotel and walked down to another place of lodging, Henry's Broadway Hotel, nearer to the boat on which he was traveling in case he was called back to it to continue his journey. It was learned that the waters of the Ohio were rapidly falling, due to lack of precipitation and to moderate temperatures. Therefore, in mid-evening Jackson responded to a request to board the Pennsylvania, and that brought out once again several thousand citizens to give a fond farewell to their new leader. Eleven p.m. was set as the departure time for the next leg of the great journey. When the crowds already in the streets heard this departure time, they immediately alerted their friends of the chance to have once again an opportunity of seeing the Hero.

The General left the Broadway Hotel at about 10:30 on the night of Saturday, January 24th, surrounded by a small group of Cincinnati's political leadership, trying to shield the President-elect—mostly without success—from his admirers. Some in the crowd again called out loud and clear, "Three Cheers for Adams!" or "Henry Clay forever." Others countered these sentiments with "Hurray for Andy!" causing Mrs. Trollope to remark on the "brutal familiarity" Americans exhibited toward their leaders.[40]

In England, no one would dare think of calling governmental officials by their first names such as "Art" (for Arthur, the Duke of Wellington, the English Prime Minister at the time). In America, as compared with England, class structures were not as rigid; therefore, a sense of equality existed between the "high" and the "low."

Mrs. Trollope's low opinion of American manners seemed to be confirmed when a "greasy fellow" broke through the crowd and directly faced Jackson. He said: "General Jackson, I suppose?"

Jackson bowed to the man, thereby signifying assent. "Why, they told me you was dead," the man continued. "No!" exclaimed Jackson, "Providence has hitherto preserved my life." The man would not let it go: "And is your wife alive, too?"[41] Under ordinary circumstances, Jackson would have caned the miscreant right then and there, but he was under careful watch by his traveling companions to control his temper.[42] Old Hickory could not orally answer such a question, so the look on his face said it all, to the extent that even the boorish man could understand. Nevertheless, the latter remarked, "Aye, I thought it was one or t'other of ye."[43] Jackson's guides wisely maneuvered him away from the scene, fearing that Jackson would inflict some harm on the inquisitive intruder.

A few minutes before 11 p.m. Jackson boarded the Pennsylvania to the sounds of bells ringing from the virtual "flotilla" of privately owned boats in the Ohio at the time. Once again, cannons went off from the boats in the river and on the shore. Jackson stood on deck waving to as many people as he could in the darkness (the only lights were gas). The Cincinnati Committee had re-charted the Fulton to accompany the Pennsylvania, all the way, its leaders claimed, to Wheeling, or even Pittsburgh, if the presidential party went that far on the Ohio.[44] Once again, the two boats were strongly lashed together by crew members, with only gas lights for illumination. A band on board the Fulton, well before leaving the Cincinnati harbor, struck up airs of the day, including patriotic songs. A Cincinnati schoolteacher, L.C. Lavin, delivered a short oration to the President-elect, telling him how happy he and his fellow Americans were that he was to be the next President.

Jackson was escorted to his quarters on the Pennsylvania by his nephew, Andrew Jackson Donelson, who had begun to maintain a "Book of Applicants," listing all those who had besought the President-elect for jobs.[45] As Jackson prepared to retire for the night, he complained to Donelson about the pain he was experiencing from shaking so many hands.[46]

Nobody got any sleep on either boat for the rest of the night, including Andrew Jackson himself, so few noticed that the Ohio River had taken a fairly sharp turn to the South. Their next major destination was Wheeling, Virginia (now a city in West Virginia), where, once again, they would check river conditions to see if the Pennsylvania in the falling level of water could make it to Pittsburgh. Otherwise, they would have to go from Wheeling on the Cumberland Road (or National Road, as it was frequently called) over the mountains and then into Washington City. Between Cincinnati and Wheeling lay Maysville and Jackson requested that the Pennsylvania and the Fulton stop there for a short while on Sunday, January 25th. During the boats' nighttime runs, they passed through several little towns and hamlets, including Augusta and Dover in Kentucky, and Ripley and Aberdeen in Ohio.

Jackson's visit to Maysville proved to be a joyous occasion: cannon firing, bells ringing, citizens turning out by the droves and shouting best wishes to the new president. Several months later, after Jackson had been in office about a year, all of this good will went down the drain. Jackson vetoed the Maysville bill, which would have brought national assistance, so the bill's sponsors said, to further segments of the Cumberland Road. But for many analysts, he did so because Maysville lay within the jurisdiction of Kentucky. And who was the best-known and most powerful man from Kentucky at this point in history? Henry Clay.

But all of that was in the future. For the time being, he definitely intended to enjoy his visit to this little picturesque town situated on the Kentucky side of the Ohio River.

On to Washington!

Chapter 9

THE END OF THE RIVER

From Cincinnati to Pittsburgh, the Pennsylvania still faced 471 river miles to go before it could deliver its famous passenger to his destination. The boat was unable to travel quite as fast as before, because it was still lashed to the Fulton, which curtailed any extra speed it might have had. More importantly, however, was the low flow of the river. Weather watchers noted that the winter of 1828-1829 was "the mildest" in the past eleven years.[1] Little precipitation in the form of rain or snow fell during January, 1829, and not until February did colder temperatures prevail.[2] On the night Jackson left Cincinnati (January 24th), morning lows barely reached below the freezing mark. During early morning the next day, January 25th, as the Pennsylvania and Fulton steamed toward Wheeling, the temperature dropped to 26 Fahrenheit, but by noon it quickly rose to 58 degrees.[3]

Some seventy-five miles upriver, although south from Cincinnati, Ohio, lay the picturesque little town of Maysville, Kentucky. Jackson decided to stop there for a while; he and the captain now decided that the Fulton should be un-lashed at Maysville instead of at Wheeling, Virginia, to allow a faster speed for the Pennsylvania. Furthermore, the low water in the Ohio River meant more obstacles for the boat: tree limbs, snags, and entire trees, all had to be carefully monitored. Also, sandbars popped up closer to the river's surface than in ordinary circumstances; little islets dotted the river, and the captain and crew had to keep a sharp eye out for them.[4] These situations discouraged night travel, further slowing down the process of getting to Wheeling and Pittsburgh.

The boats had departed Cincinnati in the midst of cannon roar, various forms of fireworks, and loud huzzahs from citizens gathered on both sides of the river. An "uncommonly fine" music band, composed of "gentlemen amateurs" went aboard the Fulton and played patriotic songs all through the remainder of the night.[5] A Jackson party committee remained on board the Fulton, as did several ladies from Cincinnati. There were great lines of people on both banks of the Ohio River (Maysville, Kentucky and Aberdeen, Ohio) waiting to get a chance to see the next President. Ladies waved their handkerchiefs and men shouted "Hurrah for Old Hickory!"

Maysville, once known as Limestone, in 1829 had a population of some 4,000 citizens. Located between the Ohio River and "high hills" which rise just behind it, Maysville was described as a "thriving" and "active town," whose major thoroughfare was the road from Lexington, Kentucky, to Chillicothe, Ohio.[6] Maysville's grounds were "sandy," containing several limestone-paved streets and brick footwalks. Among the "well built" houses were markets, a courthouse, and numerous churches.[7]

General Jackson got off the Pennsylvania at Maysville (it was now late afternoon of January 25, 1829), accompanied by the Cincinnati delegation, who shielded him as best they could from his admirers, as the "air… resounded with loud and truly warm hearted greetings."[8] Jackson went to the hotel where a Mister Carroll, hailed as one of the "first settlers" in Kentucky[9] waited to greet him. The two gentlemen talked for hours; Carroll remarked that both he and the President-elect had been "exposed to the ambushed rifle and murderous tomahawk in the wilderness, where now flourishing towns and highly cultivated districts are… to be seen."[10] The 25th being a Sunday, and with nightfall nearing, the Jackson party decided to wait until early next morning before resuming their voyage.

The next morning, January 26th, Jackson, accompanied by Major William Lewis and Major Henry Lee, "breakfasted" on board the Fulton, where Jackson's "urbane manners and kind attention" to those in his company "imparted the most heartfelt satisfaction."[11] Surrounded by a large number of "free hearted and chivalrous Kentuckians,"[12] he bade farewell to all aboard the Fulton. He met the ladies in the boat's stateroom, and then went to the upper deck where the men congregated to say goodbye to the next President of the United States. He "took leave" of each person individually, heartily shaking his hand. "All were deeply affected," said a newspaper; "almost all were in tears."[13]

Clearly, Jackson would have preferred to stay on in Maysville, among all the adulation shown to him. But there was a schedule (at least of a sort—in those days there were no specific schedules because too many unforeseen obstacles might get in the way of a boat heading from one city to another) to keep. He boarded the Pennsylvania, which was still tied tightly to the Fulton, and proceeded upriver. Once again the citizens of Aberdeen, Ohio, and Maysville, Kentucky, turned out to see Andrew Jackson, the ladies still waving their handkerchiefs, the men shouting greetings, and young children with their hands aloft, waving to the General.

About two miles upriver, the two boats stopped and their crews set about un-lashing from each other. This did not take long, for the crews were well trained in these procedures. The Pennsylvania resumed its way upriver, while the Fulton turned around back toward Maysville, with an ultimate destination of Cincinnati. All on board the Fulton watched silently as the Pennsylvania steamed out of sight, and Reverend William Burke led them in a prayer appealing for Jackson's welfare as he continued his trip to take the reins of government.

As the Fulton re-passed Maysville, the Reverend Burke preached a sermon whose theme was "The Lord hath done great things for us, whereof we are glad." The theme is from Psalms 126, verse three. The first verse spoke about the Lord freeing his followers; the second about this result bringing "laughter to our tongues," and the third showing thanks for their deliverance. The implication was clearly that Andrew Jackson, the first president from the West, was "freeing" the country of many ills. The sermon so greatly "instructed" and "edified" the Reverend's listeners that "it will long be remembered by them."[14]

Out of Maysville, with Kentucky and then Virginia on its right and Ohio on the left, the Pennsylvania steamed through such places as Trinity, Concord, Buena Vista, Greenup, Ashland, and Catlettsburg, in Kentucky; Manchester, Portsmouth, Worthington, and Ironton, in Ohio; and then joined the Virginia (now West Virginia) border at Huntington. From Huntington the Ohio River bends North, up through Gallipolis in Ohio, as well as Middleport, Pomeroy, and Marietta; and on the Virginia side Point Pleasant, Ravenswood and Parkersburg, and finally Wheeling.

As the Pennsylvania resumed its early morning trip on January 29th toward Wheeling, it passed along several towns and villages where the enthusiasm for Jackson proved not as pronounced as in previous places. One substantial reason for this reserve was that the President-elect was getting deeper into "Clay"or—as it would be called later—"Whig" country; another was the fact that neither Old Hickory nor his traveling partners showed up on deck to wave to anyone who might have lined the shores. Clearly, the sustained trip on the steamboat proved to be taking its toll as Emily Donelson wrote to her mother, in a letter that was to be mailed at Wheeling, that "our situation on the steam boat is not so pleasant as I anticipated," an especially disappointing circumstance since the boat carried no commercial—or paying—passengers, as had the Fairy; only Jackson and his traveling companions. She apparently shared a cabin with other traveling females and they were "so much crowded and are so close and confined that the least exposure is apt to give cold." To make matters worse, Jackson himself that very morning had awakened with a bad cold, causing Emily to fear adverse effects of the smallpox vaccination he received in Cincinnati. She also mentioned in this letter that the President's traveling group intended to go directly from Wheeling overland on the National Road to Washington City.[15] That may have been their intention as they plied the Ohio between Maysville, Kentucky, and Wheeling, Virginia, but they changed their minds once they got to the latter city.

Wheeling, Virginia, was suitably located to be a transportation hub. The great National Road from Baltimore crossed the Ohio River at Wheeling [the road's western terminus at this time was Zanesville, Ohio] giving the city a double-edged advantage in reference to trade and commerce.[16] Its population of some 5,000 people, lived in 600 houses, went to two churches and shopped at one bookstore. Also "several inns" in the area drew the comment that "some...are highly respectable."[17] The citizens of Wheeling had also practically deified Henry Clay for what he had done in getting the National (or Cumberland) Road run through their city. Jackson's visit, therefore, created as much polite curiosity as any kind of warm welcome.

Wheeling had been founded by twenty-one-year-old Ebenezer Zane of Virginia in 1769. He stood on a hill that overlooked good farmlands adjacent to the Ohio River, and he also saw several fords by which one could cross the stream so that one could easily benefit from the fertile soils on both sides. His brothers, Jonathan and Silas, came with him and the three decided that this was the place they wanted to settle.[18] Just a year after Ebenezer's claim, word spread about the rich, fertile soil in the area, and hundreds of "claims seekers" converged on the spot. The English, of course, still laid claim to this area, and generally referred to it as the "Western Frontier." Years later, during the American Revolution, the Zanes became famous for defending Wheeling, or Fort Henry as it was called, both from British and Indian attacks.[19]

In the years following the War for Independence, Wheeling became famous, being located at the head of steam navigation on the Ohio, and it boasted the busiest road in the country, as western and southern politicians and thousands of businessmen and ordinary travelers came through it each year.[20] One of the dignitaries who passed through was the Marquis de Lafayette; his visit in 1825 certainly got more attention than the 1829 stopover by Andrew Jackson. In fact, the press in Wheeling seemed reluctant to mention Jackson at all. There were two leading newspapers in Wheeling at the time. *The Virginia Statesman* wrote: "Gen. Andrew Jackson, president elect of the United States arrived here this morning on board the steam boat Pennsylvania. He departed for Pittsburgh about 10 o'clock on the same boat."[21] *The Wheeling Gazette*, almost as terse as the *Statesman*, gave this notice: "On Wednesday last, the Steam Boat Pennsylvania having on board General Jackson, touched at this place on her way to Pittsburgh. During the few hours the boat remained, the General was visited by a large number of our citizens."[22]

Almost certainly these "citizens" were not followers of Henry Clay, the idol in the city. Again, probably polite curiosity brought them out rather than any wild enthusiasms about the President-elect. However, one group wanted to see Jackson personally and present him with a glass flask, as they had done when Lafayette visited four years before. They sent word to the General that they wanted to show him that he was the "political choice" of at least a part of the communities surrounding Wheeling;[23] the place was not completely a "hot-bed" of Clayism.

Old Hickory went ashore briefly to receive the flask offered to him by this group of his followers. One side of the flask depicted Jackson himself in a semi-circle; on the reverse there was an American eagle's head turned to the left, with seven bars on his breast and wings partly raised, with the left one foreshortened. In the eagle's left talon was a thunderbolt and in the right a large olive branch, under which were six cannon balls. Above the eagle were seven large five-pointed stars. In the lower part of the panel was the inscription "Knox & McKee" (the makers of the flask) and in the upper part was the word "Wheeling," depicting the place where it was offered (and also made) to the President-elect. The whole product was pale green, with "yellow tones."[24] Jackson graciously accepted the flask but left it with the Wheeling group, apparently desiring not to add to the heavy loads of materials he already had with him; this was necessary since at Pittsburgh he would be obliged to transfer everything to a coach, which would undoubtedly have less room for cargo than the Pennsylvania.[25]

While the Pennsylvania was docked at Wheeling, one of Jackson's traveling companions, Major William B. Lewis, wrote a lengthy letter for newspapers giving a recap of their journey so far and their intentions for its remainder. He recounted the stopovers at Louisville, Cincinnati, and Maysville, and the grand receptions President-elect Jackson and his group received. At the time of this letter, January 28, 1829, the Pennsylvania had been docked at Wheeling for about two hours and was expected to leave for Pittsburgh in one hour, "provided we are not detained by ice or the want of water," in the Ohio River.[26] From Pittsburgh, Lewis claimed, the presidential party would go straight to Washington ("Little Washington"), Pennsylvania, and then "directly" to the capital. He re-emphasized Jackson's reasons for wanting to enter Washington, D.C. "without parade or ceremony," the first being a principle of Republicanism, and secondly, respect for his "present state of feelings," since he was still in mourning for Rachel.[27] Furthermore, it was impossible, the major said, even to give an estimate other than "sometime in February" about when the presidential party would reach Washington. "He [Jackson] is in pretty good health," Lewis reported, and has stood the journey so far, very well."[28]

Showing that the presidential counselors were still undecided about the best route out of Wheeling, Lewis added a postscript to his letter, stating that "since writing the above" letter, "it has been determined to decline going to Pittsburgh." It was doubtful that they could get there by water, since the Ohio's levels continued to lower. From Wheeling overland to Washington City was about 215 miles; from Pittsburgh overland it was some 200 miles, so the difference in mileage was minimal. Nevertheless, after this postscript was added, the General and his advisors once again picked Pittsburgh as their upriver destination; it was roughly sixty river miles to that Pennsylvania city.[29]

Why the indecision? First, the citizens of Wheeling had not known exactly when the President-elect would arrive—or, indeed, if he would even stop in their city—so no livery arrangements had been made for teams of horses or for carriages. Though there were many inns, hotels, and taverns outside of Wheeling on the developing National Road, no distinct overnight reservations had been made for Old Hickory and his traveling partners. The weather in late January took a turn for the worse, freezing roadways and making horses' footing precarious. Also, the Jackson party probably wanted to get out of Wheeling and its environs as quickly as possible, seeing as how their presence had been frowned upon by large portions of the populace.[30]

On the other hand, the committee in Pittsburgh already had reservations for the visiting dignitaries—at the Mansion House Hotel—[31] so if they could just get a "few more miles" upriver, they would be assured of comfortable resting places before continuing their odyssey to the capital city. Captain Kierstedt of the Pennsylvania was willing to take a chance with the river, and so was Jackson. If they were stopped by water conditions en route to Pittsburgh, they could, of course, disembark and take the rest of the trip by coach. After being in Wheeling for a little over two hours, the Pennsylvania steamed out into the river at 10 a.m. on January 28, 1829, and proceeded toward Pittsburgh,[32] inching its way because of low water and all the problems that came with it.

In a way the segment from Wheeling to Pittsburgh turned out to be the most challenging of the entire trip. On previous legs of the journey (going down the Cumberland, for example) Jackson's boat had sometimes got up to ten miles an hour and had been able to travel through the night. Although the Pennsylvania steamed through the night it was only at five or six miles per hour, or less. This slow pace was necessitated by the low water with its attendant problem of tree limbs, snags, high-rising sandbars and other debris. Shortly after dawn on January 29th, the usual "mountains of heads" showed up as thousands of people began to appear on both river banks, a sight that continued on into Pittsburgh. Two boats, the Delaware—lavishly decorated in laurel—and the Shamroz, steamed down the river to meet the Pennsylvania. Both of these boats were lighter than the Pennsylvania, so they ran in front of the heavier ship, behind it, to its sides, and made several circles in the river while celebratory cannon fire came from the shore. On board the Delaware was the "committee of arrangements," to see to the President-elect's comfort while he was in Pittsburgh.[33] The two boats lined up on the Pennsylvania's bow and led the big ship to Pittsburgh's Market Street wharf where, a few minutes after docking, Jackson walked ashore.[34]

On the dock the Committee was waiting for the President-elect, and standing behind this committee were "huge hordes of spectators."[35] The crowds became so immense that the "reception committee feared they would inadvertently tumble the President-elect and his companions into the muddy river."[36] In fact, the General was "literally carried" on the shoulders of numerous intense Jackson supporters to the home of a Mr. McDonald, where he stayed—speaking cordially and happily with everyone he met—until the mortified Reception Committee caught up with him, and escorted him to his hotel.[37]

As at some of the previous stopovers, Jackson decided to walk from the boat to Mansion House, the hotel reserved for him by the local Committee. This hotel was only a quarter of a mile away from the wharf, but it took Jackson and his party over an hour to get to it.[38] He insisted on shaking all the hands offered to him—and these seemed to be in the tens of thousands—and sometimes speak to citizens who lined his route to the hotel. One observer noted that, although there were "hurrahs," "huzzahs," and shouts of "Jackson forever," there were no fifes and drums or any "pomp or parades,"[39] in keeping with Jackson's wish that there be no lavish displays of either affection or disapproval; after all, he was still in mourning for Rachel. Apparently, the Jacksonian press in Pittsburgh did not give much publicity to Jackson's arrival, although the President-elect was extremely popular in that city, especially among such ethnic groups as the Scotch-Irish (he was, himself, descended from the Scotch-Irish). *The Pittsburgh Statesman* addressed the lack of coverage by "democratic" newspapers: "Although it might not be agreeable to our Jackson friends," the paper asserted, "that we should give the particulars of the General's visit to this city," it hoped that it could "without offence [sic]" report that Jackson arrived on Steamboat Pennsylvania on his way to Washington City.[40]

The paper noted that his arrival was met with "loud acclamations" and "feelings of cheerful enthusiasm." The General appeared to be "highly gratified" at these "greetings,"[41] showing a "buoyant" spirit, and "graciously" bowing to the multitudes. Although his head was "frosted even to whiteness," and his body exhibited "marks of emaciation," brought on, supposedly, by "anxiety, care, and age," Jackson's demeanor was one of strength and resoluteness, sometimes striding faster and with more confidence than many of those younger people accompanying him. He treated both friends and opponents equally with "unmarked kindness and cordiality" to all who approached him. He was "hospitably entertained" by some of Pittsburgh's leading citizens who, after Jackson rested up some, escorted him on a tour of the city's business and manufacturing centers.[42]

He did not, however, ignore the common elements, either in Pittsburgh or in any other cities he visited on his way to Washington City. At the Mansion House Hotel, where the Jackson party stayed until Saturday, January 31st, a special room was set aside by management for Jackson to receive well-wishing callers and supplicants for government jobs. One of his visitors was a veteran of the War of 1812 who had been at New Orleans with Jackson on January 8, 1815, the day of the American victory against the British. A cannon had exploded on this veteran as he tried to fire it, and as a consequence he lost both of his arms. After several minutes of conversation, it was clear that the Old General was emotionally affected by the story of his comrade-in-arms. He folded up a banknote and gave it to the veteran. Later, it was discovered that it was a one hundred dollar bill![43]

In Pittsburgh, Jackson's long river voyage to become Chief of State came to an end. Three major rivers flowed through Pittsburgh: the Allegheny and the Monongahela emptied into the Ohio. Jackson gazed upon all three of these great watery thoroughfares, and undoubtedly marveled that he had made the journey in such a relatively short time. He was vaguely aware that the country was just on the verge of a transportation "revolution," with trains soon to catch up with river boat and coach travel.

For the time being, however, he savored his presence in friendly and hospitable Pittsburgh, and looked forward to the next and final leg of his journey. He and his party had now traveled some 1,128 river miles from the Hermitage to Pittsburgh, and they had about 200 land miles to go before arrival at their final destination. During the two nights they stayed at Pittsburgh's Mansion House Hotel, they rested and regained their stamina; therefore, at noon on Saturday, January 31st, Jackson left in a plain carriage drawn by two ordinary horses, accompanied by a few Pennsylvania militiamen, and a "cavalcade" of citizens who planned to accompany him and his party[44] as far as Washington, Pennsylvania, a few miles down the road from Pittsburgh. One newspaper, the *Pittsburgh Mercury*, summed up Jackson's visit; citizens had greeted him with the "language of the heart." Jackson had shown a "vigorous mind, inflexibility of purpose... blended with... softness." The paper closed its article about Jackson's visit by exclaiming that, "It was impossible that the spectator should not love and venerate Andrew Jackson!"[45] This statement, and ones like it, must have caused anti-Jacksonians all over the country to utter loud guffaws, even though such assertions were mostly true.

Chief Justice John Marshall administers the presidential Oath of Office to Andrew Jackson, March 4, 1829.

Chapter 10

Mr. President

All along the journey from Nashville on the Cumberland to Pittsburgh on the Ohio, many spectators crowding banks and piers seemed surprised or even shocked to see Andrew Jackson wave to them or step ashore. Some were relieved at the sight of him; others were downright disappointed. "He is alive!" muttered the multitudes who had turned out to see him pass through their areas.

Few citizens in the twenty-four states knew the location of the President-elect. The only information they had about him was that he was on a big boat somewhere on a river heading for Washington City to take over the government. Newspapers that recounted his progress were frequently over a week old—or more—when readers acquired them, so news about Jackson was already out-dated by the time citizens read accounts of his travels.

They had, of course, heard about Rachel's tragic and untimely death, and it was understandable that some could confuse Andrew with her, and therefore believe the stories they heard that the President-elect had died on his way to Washington. An earlier rumor had stated that Jackson, being so sorrowful about losing Rachel, had resigned the Presidency-elect. Now this new rumor of his death began to spread throughout the land, causing consternation among a large proportion of the body politic. Jackson's first inkling of his "death" had come at Cincinnati when the boor asked him about Rachel (recounted in Chapter Eight). For the rest of the trip this rumor and the one about his resignation seemed to grow with every mile traveled.

The origins of his "death" had more than a little foolishness attached to them, and definitely showed the gullibility and wishful thinking of some people—particularly the General's opponents—in believing hearsay and newspaper misprints. The first instance of the President-elect's "death" came from Nashville, where an undocumented letter noted that Jackson planned to leave the Hermitage on January 20, 1829, for Washington City, but did on January 19th.[1] The recipient of the letter (unnamed in newspaper reports) read the word did as died,[2] with its rippling effects causing great consternation among the citizenry, exciting "the most anxious sensations among all classes of people…"[3] and numerous politicians. Many newspapers noted the generally frail conditions of the General as he was en route, but at the same time they stressed that they were not life-threatening.

As if the Nashville rumor were not enough, it re-emerged as the President-elect steamed through Ohio. There was another letter, this one from Columbus, Ohio, written by an unnamed person to Mr. Ruggles, a member of the Ohio Legislature who forwarded it to a confidant in Washington.[4] It stated that on January 27th, the General was "very ill," and on the 28th, he supposedly died.[5] Jackson, of course, did not go through Columbus, and this caused many people to be wary of such reports. The accounts of his visit to Cincinnati, south of Columbus, were closely reviewed with reference to illnesses of various sorts, but not of death. Such comparisons caused some newspapers to speculate that these rumors were deliberately spread by the opposition party to foment uneasiness and even turmoil throughout the land. It was now February, with a new president scheduled to be installed on March 4th. If the President-elect was not available, who would be?

The undocumented Columbus letter stated that General Jackson had stopped on the Ohio to visit Chillicothe, a few miles away from the river. While there, Jackson was treated to warm greetings and a full dinner. The letter writer said that Jackson "dined" at Chillicothe; apparently, the recipient omitted the 'n,' making it read that Jackson had "died."[6] Whoever it was told a friend who told a friend and before long, there was a full-fledged rumor that a constitutional crisis was at hand, because the Constitution did not address the problem of what would happen if the President-elect died before taking office.[7] Some observers saw this rumor as an effort to keep John Quincy Adams in Office or, if not, perhaps to elevate Secretary of State Henry Clay, to the position of Chief Executive.

The "death" rumor instigated a full-blown debate among newspapers in the United States about who would be the new President if Andrew Jackson died before March 4, 1829. Interestingly enough, some saw the hand of Vice-President John C. Calhoun—who had long aspired to the presidency—in these matters. The rumor, said one paper, had "elicited…rancorous hostility" to Calhoun who, in every regard, "is even less acceptable than the Chieftain himself."[8] None of these papers, however, ascribed any particular motives to Mr. Calhoun. The electoral votes were scheduled to be counted on February 11th. Did Calhoun or any other person believe they might manipulate the Electoral College to change their votes from Jackson to another candidate? Did he believe the House of Representatives might meet in emergency session before March 4th, and elect him or someone other than Jackson? The newspapers which wrote on these concerns were long on innuendos and short on explanations and assessments.

Apparently, many citizens who heard of Jackson's "death" believed that the country now had no Chief Executive at all, and that the United States was on the verge of anarchical insurrection. Newspapers rushed to quell these fears by saying that John Quincy Adams was still the President—at least until March 4th. It was at that date that a real constitutional crisis might arise.[9] Even if under the circumstances, Mr. Adams might possibly be eligible to be considered by the House of Representatives to continue his office after March 4th, his supporters defended him by saying that "he would not accept the [continued] Presidency on such terms."[10]

The case before the government and the people was one of omission in the Constitution, meaning that the Founders had not considered what would happen if a President-elect died before assuming the duties of the Executive Office. Therefore, in this matter, many observers believed, the Constitution must be interpreted in its spirit rather than its letter;[11] if this were done, John C. Calhoun, who had been J.Q. Adams' Vice-President as well as now becoming Jackson's Vice-President, would be sworn in as President.

But, it was argued, John C. Calhoun had not run for President in the 1828 election; he had run for Vice-President. On the other hand, John Quincy Adams had run for President, coming in second to Jackson with eighty-three electoral votes to Jackson's 178. But if Jackson were deceased, all the electoral votes that had been cast for him would be lost and, according to this opinion, ought to go to the candidate who came in second. The person who received the second largest "confidence of the people" was President Adams, not Vice-President Calhoun.[12] This situation led many to believe that Adams should continue for a second term, a suggestion that evoked immediate negative responses, including one that threatened "the peace of the nation" if carried out.[13]

Jackson was mostly aware of all the rumors surrounding his journey to the White House. He was more disturbed by beliefs that he had "resigned" his office of President-elect than by those that claimed he had "died." For Jackson to have resigned would have been totally out of character for him, and he was incensed that anyone would think him capable of such an act. His traveling party shielded him to a considerable extent from the hearsays. They knew how temperamental he could be, and they guarded against any negative incidents along the way that would undoubtedly create additional controversies about the soon-to-be Chief Executive.

Heading out of Pittsburgh toward Washington, Pennsylvania (generally called "Little Washington" to distinguish it from Washington, D.C.), the Jackson party actually retraced on land what they had already traveled on river. On the Ohio they went upriver, towards the North; on the road[14] to Washington, they went almost due South.

His coach could travel about twenty-five miles in a twelve-hour period if the roads were passable; coaches, unlike river boats, generally did not travel at night. It had been snowing in Pittsburgh on the day of Jackson's arrival, and the weather remained cold as he continued his trip to the capitol city. "Little Washington," about thirty miles south of Pittsburgh, "received" Jackson with "some show of ceremony."[15] This "coolness" in "Little Washington" proved somewhat surprising because so many of its inhabitants were, like Jackson, descendants of the Scotch-Irish. Perhaps it had to do with the fact that Washington, Pennsylvania, had been one of the flash points in the famous (or infamous) "Whiskey Rebellion" of 1794, which was still within living memory for many of its citizens. The government in 1794, while George Washington was President, sent troops into the area to enforce excise taxes; ever since that time, the residents of Western Pennsylvania had distrusted government and its symbols, especially the Chief Executive. It was also getting late in the day when Jackson's party arrived in Washington, Pennsylvania, and it still had about ten miles to go before its scheduled stop for the night.

The travelers continued on, now east of "Little Washington," to an establishment known as "Hill's Tavern." Built in 1794 by Stephen Hill, it almost immediately became a popular stopover for travelers. Made of stone dug up from the site where it was built, it contained twenty rooms (and still does) which could accommodate nineteen guests, one of whom in early 1829 was Andrew Jackson, on his way to become the seventh president of the United States.[16] Hill had the incredibly good fortune for his place of business to be located on a road that later became a part of the "Cumberland" Road or, as it came to be called, the "National Road." This road assured a booming business to any establishment located on its path, or even in its environs.

Century Inn, Scenery Hill, Pennsyvania, standing as it did in 1829, when Jackson stayed for two nights on his Inaugural trip. It was named Hill's Tavern at the time. Photo by the author.

The Jackson party arrived at Hill's Tavern late at nearly midnight on January 31, 1829. The Appalachians lay in front of them, and they did not particularly want to cross them at nighttime. Advance riders had alerted the staff to the imminent arrival of important guests; the kitchens stayed open so that they would have a good meal if they wanted. Jackson declined, because he was still feverish from the cold he had caught coming out of Cincinnati, so he went straight to the suite, which had been reserved for him.

He may have regretted later that he missed Hill's Tavern "groaning board," usually presented at the establishment's "Whiskey Rebellion" offering. It consisted of curry-corn chowder, baked turkey, Virginia ham, Yankee red flannel hash (made from mixture of corn beef and vegetables), Yorkshire meat pie (probably an import from England), and pippins (apples) with sausage, and onion pie. An array of desserts offered carrot custards, yams (sweet potatoes) with chestnuts and apples, and "tipsy squire" (a non-alcoholic dish of flour, milk, and sweeteners). It is likely, however, that on his second night at Hill's, the President-elect did partake of these delicious foods.[17]

The next day they decided to stay a second night at Hill's Tavern. They were still tired from the festivities in Pittsburgh and then from the carriage ride to Washington, Pennsylvania. They needed rest and some time to catch up on paperwork. Besides, February 1st being a Sunday, Jackson realized that criticisms would be leveled against him if he and his party traveled by coach on a Sabbath.

Since they needed fresh horses, Jackson switched to a spacious four-wheeled carriage, drawn by "four beautiful grays."[18] As they started out in the early morning of Monday, February 2nd, literally thousands of people converged on the grounds of Hill's Tavern to see this famous departure, and also on both sides of the road leading out of the little village of Scenery Hill. Pennsylvania Governor John Andrew Shulze authorized additional militia to travel with the President-elect, not so much to protect him from any violence, but to keep the masses at a respectable distance, many of whom crowded his coach, just wanting to say something to him or, better yet, shake his hand.

The weather was mild on this second day of February (fifty

degrees high and forty degrees low),[19] and this part of the National Road in fairly good condition, so the travelers made good time. The National Road had been the brainchild of Albert Gallatin,[20] a Swiss-born congressman and later Secretary of the Treasury, who, like President George Washington, wanted a "wide highway" to run from the Chesapeake Bay area to a rapidly developing St. Louis, on the Mississippi River. Construction began in 1808 at Cumberland, Maryland, (which caused the thoroughfare also to be called the "Cumberland Road"), while Thomas Jefferson was in the presidential office.

In following years, the road was constructed in fits and starts because of a controversy over internal improvements: should the federal government pay to build roads or should the states finance them? Often, by the time one Congress and President had authorized an additional section of the road, the previous sections had largely deteriorated, even grown up in weeds. Everyone wanted a National Road, it seemed, if only it went through their town, and many words were written and spoken that supported local options. Various newspapers printed mixed feelings on the subject.

In early 1829, when the road's western terminus was Zanesville, Ohio, the *Cincinnati Chronicle* editorialized that future cities to be favored should include Springfield, Yellow Spring, Xenia, Lebanon, and Cincinnati—all in Ohio; and on into Frankfort in Kentucky and Nashville in Tennessee.[21] The *Daily Gazette* reported that a group of Ohio engineers recommended that the road go from Zanesville to Chillicothe, Ohio; then to Maysville and Lexington in Kentucky; and finally to Nashville. Finally, the road should be constructed from Nashville to New Orleans.[22] In reality, however, the road to St. Louis continued to be favored by the Washington lawmakers.

Interposed on these suggestions about where the National Road should go was the all important question: Is the National Road constitutional in the first place? Some politicians said "Yes," while others defiantly answered "No." The *Banner-Whig* in Nashville asserted that while most Americans seemed to support ideas of general internal improvements, there were some objectionable issues. A major one concerned the taking of private property through the concept of eminent domain (that is, arguing that the rights of the public supersede the rights of an individual) must be carefully monitored and carried out legally, through court orders. Also there was a proposal that toll gates be erected at several places along the road, a proposition opposed even by many who supported the road in the first place. "The chief error" said the *Banner-Whig*, in the matter of toll gates, "is the assumption that... Congress has the right to construct this road."[23]

Presidents, as well as Congresses, varied in their opinions about the National Road. Jefferson, although he claimed to be a "strict constructionist" of the Constitution, authorized the first activities on the Road. James Madison believed that the entire question of internal improvements should be subjected to a Constitutional Amendment. James Monroe and John Quincy Adams seemed to be more friendly to internal improvements than their predecessors. But Andrew Jackson, currently in 1829 using the services of the National Road, would become notorious for his vetoes of internal improvement bills. He believed, as did Madison, that a Constitutional Amendment should settle the legality of internal improvements as well as the vast inconsistencies of funding it. That he traveled on a Road in early 1829, construction of large parts of which he would later delay, was one of the many ironies about Andrew Jackson and his career.

The barouche coach that carried him out of Hill's Tavern on the 2nd probably had his slave Charles from the Hermitage at the reins of the four grays. Someone had painted "General Jackson" on the sides of the carriage, to let people know who was passing through their communities, as though they needed to be told. Jackson, as with the Fairy from the Hermitage to Louisville, was offered free passage. He declined because he did not want to be "beholden" to any private interests, but he did allow members of his traveling party to use the complimentary travel.[24]

Jackson seemed reluctant to leave the Pittsburgh-Washington areas. After departing from Hill's Tavern, his entourage headed for Brownsville, an important center for flatboat and keelboat construction.[25] He slowed down his presidential procession for at least two reasons.

The President-elect had been through Brownsville several times. In a prior visit, in 1828, he had complained to its citizens about the "corrupt bargain" of 1824, which put John Quincy Adams into the White House and installed Henry Clay in the State Department. Perhaps now in 1829 Jackson wanted some personal glory in his presidential election—although he was not a gloating type, and besides, his mood was still somber because of Rachel's death—to show both friends and foes how the country had changed in the past four years.

He and his fellow travelers checked in at George Gibson's Inn, located on Church Street in Brownsville.[26] Jackson received, of course, the best suite in the house—and as at Hill's Tavern—was offered the "most sumptuous" meal the chef and his staff could prepare. The meal, long in the making, consisted of several entrees of roasted beef and pork, to be followed by numerous desserts.

The President-elect, however, "amazed" the chef and kitchen personnel. He said "ham and eggs."[27]

"But Mr. President," the chef countered, "there must be some mistake. You surely don't want ham and eggs."

"Yes sir, that's what I ordered," Jackson sternly replied, "and that's what I want."[28] A server rushed to the kitchen to arrange a special presidential meal (he usually had eggs lightly scrambled). Probably no one at Gibson's Inn knew of the delicate nature of Jackson's digestive system; ham and eggs was one of the few dishes he could enjoy without fearing the consequences.

An hour or so after this early supper, Andrew Jackson received a visitation by a committee of the Lodge of Hope and Good Intentions at Ft. Burd, "commonly known as Brownsville," Free and Accepted Masons. Since Jackson was a mason and since the Lodge was meeting that very night, the members could not allow this opportunity of having Jackson as a guest to pass by.[29] The committee escorted "Brother Andrew" to the meeting hall, where he was the guest of honor. As he was introduced to each member, he bowed gracefully to him, extending his hand in fellowship. Though the minutes of the meeting did refer to him as the "President-elect," many of the members—much to his delight—called him simply "Brother Andrew."[30] When the meeting ended the same committee that had called on him escorted him back to the Gibson Inn where, a while later, he adjusted the picture of his beloved Rachel so that she would be facing him through the night, he fell into a peaceful sleep.

Jackson decided next morning, February 3rd, to send two horseback riders on ahead to Washington City to report that he would be arriving around February 10th or 11th. His party was still around 200 miles away, and if the weather held steady, they could reach the capitol city within another week or so. The two riders, Robert Hays and Andrew Jackson, Jr., both Rachel's nephews, set off at once from Brownsville toward Maryland and the District of Columbia. Along the way, when stopping to rest their horses or change them for new ones, they informed the owners of inns, hotels, taverns and sometimes private residences (though none of these were in abundance through the mountainous regions) that the President-elect was on his way and might want to stop off at their establishment for a while, a pleasing proposition to most of them.

Another reason why Jackson and his group took their time passing through "Little" Washington and Brownsville and then Uniontown, was that he did not want to get to Washington City before the certification of electoral votes by the Senate. It was scheduled to count the votes on Wednesday, February 11th. Jackson did not want to arrive until he had received all 178 electoral votes to which he was entitled following the November, 1828, presidential election.[31] Of course, he knew that the electoral count in the Senate was usually a mere formality, but with the political bitterness of the day, he feared that his enemies might still make an effort to manipulate matters to get another term for President Adams. Thus, he believed his entry into Washington before the electoral votes had been counted "would seem a little awkward."[32]

In the meantime, he and his group continued on their way, with the next major stop to be in Uniontown, Pennsylvania. It was the "most flourishing town west of the mountains outside Pittsburgh and Wheeling."[33] A popular stopover for travelers, the National Road as it passed through Uniontown was "thickly studded with public houses on both sides and from end to end."[34]

Jackson had passed through Uniontown before, going to Washington City and coming back. Although his favorite hotel was the Brunswick, once he arrived in the city in early afternoon on February 4th, he was escorted by a "cavalcade of citizens"[35] to the Union Hotel.[36] The proprietress was Mrs. McCleary, and she and her staff had prepared a "sumptuous dinner" of several entrees for the President-elect. Unlike in Brownsville, where he had only wanted eggs and ham, he "partook"[37] of this meal with great enthusiasm.[38]

Jackson's travel caravan started out from Uniontown at about 6 p.m., once again heading east. One locality near Uniontown that he and his party had to travel through must have galled the old General considerably. This was the Henry Clay Township, established in June, 1822, by Fayette County, Pennsylvania, authorities. His companions might have withheld this information from the President-elect. It would have been well in character for him, however, to rush through an area named for his old nemesis from Kentucky. He was perhaps ameliorated, at least to some degree, when the group—still outside Uniontown—passed by the Mount Washington Presbyterian Church, which had also been established in 1822. Though he was not a Presbyterian, he knew that both his mother and father had been, so there was a warm feeling for the structure and its congregation.

Their intention was to stay on the road for the next four nights and days, so that at around two or three miles per hour, they could be in a good position to reach Washington by February 10th or 11th. They could travel at nighttime, at least a part of it, even over the mountains, by lantern light affixed to all the coaches, following instructions of advance riders, who went ahead to check their path for obstacles and dangers. (If saddle horses were available, some of the men just for the joy of it—rode horseback during much of each day).[39] When citizens along the way heard that the President-elect's arrival was imminent, many gathered on the roadsides with their lanterns, providing more than enough light for the entourage to see.

Actually, the mountains were not all that formidable. They rarely got above 3,000 feet in altitude and the steepness was about a five to six percent gradient. When going downhill, a clever coach driver could manipulate the brakes and speed to match the gait of the horses, who could either trot down the decline or even walk, without having the strain of pulling a coach. Of course, they were taxed on the ascents; nevertheless there were numerous restful places along the way for both animals and humans. For one thing, when getting to the top of a mountain, there were frequently long, level ridges that produced relatively easy traveling conditions. Under these circumstances, and with unusually warm weather for that time of year (although, however, fogs were frequent), the coaches could make good time. Some of these ridges were 30 to 40 miles in length, and these were always welcomed by the travelers. The group passed over such mountains, and took advantage of their ridges as Big Savage, Negro and Green River in Pennsylvania, and Polish Mountain, in Maryland.

They went through areas that were close to several little communities such as Claysville, Waynesburg, Cannonsburg and Chalk Hill, in Pennsylvania, and Grantsville, Swanton, Hancock, and Frostburg in Maryland. Since inns and taverns were not as plentiful in the mountains as elsewhere, it was not unknown for Jackson's traveling group to stop at private homes for new supplies, resting horses and meeting citizens. Many times these good mountain people came out onto the road itself bearing food and drink (sometimes the latter was corn whiskey, for which they knew Jackson had a fondness) to serve to the passers-by; always received gratefully by the travelers. The hospitality of the mountains was manifest to the President-elect and his traveling companions.

Jackson's four-wheeled coach was outfitted with a bed, which gave him a modicum of comfort; he had experienced worse conditions in the field on military missions. A charcoal brazier tempered the twenty-degree weather,[40] and the ever-present chamber pot comforted him throughout the nights. There was no "press corps" accompanying the presidential party, so newspaper accounts of his journey between Uniontown, Pennsylvania, and Hagerstown, Maryland, were scanty. The Pennsylvania militiamen appointed by the governor were still guarding the cavalcade, but neither President John Quincy Adams nor any other branch of the federal government offered assistance in Jackson's trip. He was, as far as official Washington was concerned, on his own. The traveling party did stop from time to time for the rest that their coaches could not give them, to refresh or get new horses and to partake of the hospitality offered to them along the way.

By Saturday, February 7th, they had safely passed through the Appalachian Mountains and arrived in the vicinity of Hagerstown, Maryland, where—much to the relief of many in the entourage, especially the women—they decided to linger for a while. They stopped late in the day just west of Hagerstown, at Indian Spring, where they "supped" with numerous citizens of the area.[41] Escorted to Bell's Tavern after the meal, they stayed both Saturday and Sunday nights.

Hagerstown citizens, while mostly friendly to Jackson, did have detractors. Some residents greeted him with copies of "coffin bills," referring to the six militiamen Jackson had condemned to death in his campaign against the Creek Indians in Alabama territory during the War of 1812; much of the country had always thought these soldiers had been "unjustly slaughtered."[42] A few from Hagerstown even blamed him for a horrible accident that had happened a few days after his election in November, 1828. On November 13th, several Jacksonians celebrated his victory by firing off cannons. Two pieces of artillery exploded; a fragment struck and killed George Bowers, "severing his head from his body and hurling it a distance of a hundred yards into an adjoining field."[43] If Jackson had not been elected, some argued, the cannon fire would not have occurred, and Mr. Bowers would have been spared his grisly departure. So, it was all Jackson's fault!

After the supper at Indian Spring and checking into Bell Tavern, the President-elect and his party (now consisting of Andrew Jackson Donelson and Emily and their small son; Major Lee and Lady; Mrs. and Miss Love, Miss Eastin and Major Lewis) spent a restful Saturday night. Jackson was up early, as usual, on Sunday morning, February 8th.

Since it was the Sabbath he knew it would not be advisable to travel, so he stated his wish to go to church. He asked the landlord at the Bell to direct him to the nearest Presbyterian Church, saying that his father, Andrew Jackson, Sr., while in Ireland, had been a member of that denomination. The tavern keeper was not a church-goer, so he summoned Elder John Robertson of the Associate Reformed Presbyterian Church of Hagerstown to come to the Inn and accompany the distinguished guest to services. Robertson, of course, was pleased to do so; and so were hundreds of others. When they heard that Jackson was walking to church, hundreds of people "crowded to see the great democratic leader."[44] Robertson and his "helpers" escorted Jackson and his entire party to the newly-built Presbyterian Church on South Potomac Street (the present site of Hagerstown Independent Church).[45]

When the distinguished guests were seated, the Reverend Matthew Fuller introduced them to the congregation, amid murmurs of welcome. The main song for the morning was "Heavenly Father, Hear Thy Children," the words for which "were from the Adams-Burtnianski hymn, 'God is With Us Everywhere.'"[46] Then the good Reverend preached a sermon that, to say the least, was ironic for the occasion. His sermon's theme—from First Peter 5:8 was "Be sober, be vigilant; because your adversary the devil, as a roaring lion, walketh about, seeking whom he may devour."[47] Afterwards, Reverend Fuller defended his choice of topics by saying that he had chosen this text long before he knew the "Lion" would be in his company. For his part, the Old General seemed to be amused.

Throughout the afternoon of the 8th, Jackson greeted literally hundreds of guests who came to Bell Tavern to meet with him, most just simply to be able to tell their grandchildren about it. One poor man from the local almshouse, however, showed up and earnestly entreated the President-elect for a new suit of clothes, with a few extra shirts. It turned out that this was a hoax; a local attorney had drawn up the "petition" for help from Jackson, expecting it would be denied (as, indeed, it was), so he could show his colleagues how unfeeling Jackson and his followers actually were.[48] This "petition" was the exception; most of Hagerstown greeted Jackson "not as a conquering hero, but as a plain Republican citizen."[49]

Early the next day, Monday the 9th, Jackson walked over to the city's town hall to view a painting by William Dunlap entitled "The Bearing of the Cross."[50] Jackson liked the painting for its religious connotations (his mother, Elizabeth, always wanted him to become a preacher; his devout wife, Rachel, always tried to get him to join a church) and because he had met Dunlap a few years earlier and liked both the man and his work.

His coach was waiting when he returned from Town Hall, and so were his traveling companions. One newspaper urged the crowds to accompany Jackson "to the adjoining county [Frederick] or as much further as they might think proper."[51]

The meaning of this "advice" was unmistakable; however, it offered a minority view. Most citizens wished him God-speed on his way to the capitol and hoped, along with the *Hagerstown Mail*, that his presidency would be as great "to the American people at large" as his victory in New Orleans had been to the American generation of several years before.[52] He continued to shake so many hands that some in his group had to remind him of schedules; climbing into his carriage, he turned once again to the crowd, waved at them, and said, "To do justice to all."[53]

The weather was sunny and the temperatures stayed between 30 and 38 degrees. Out of Hagerstown, the presidential cavalcade traveled through Funkstown to Boonsboro; over South Mountain to Middletown; then over Braddock Mountain into Frederick, Maryland.[54] Jackson's arrival was announced "by the firing of cannon and the ringing of bells,"[55] but the "noise and confusion" was too much for some people. Frederick was predominantly anti-Jackson at the time, having gone for Adams in the recent presidential election; as at Wheeling, there was no love lost between the good citizens of Frederick, Maryland, and Andrew Jackson.[56] The editor of the town's leading newspaper, the *Herald*, refused to participate in any celebratory greetings; he did, however, watch as the President-elect was "dragged,"—apparently meaning "rushed"—along the street in "the most unhandsome [sic] style."[57]

A Frederick citizen, Jacob Engelbrecht, started the entry in his daily diary with: "Jackson's Come!" He was awed at how "the natives did Gaze at him," including himself, who "went with the current."[58] The traveling party went to the Talbott Hotel, where they checked in, hoping to get a good night's rest in preparation for the final leg of their journey, which would take them into Washington City within the next two days.

Jackson still intended to arrive in Washington without any fanfare, and as close to the counting of electoral votes as was possible. City officials and leaders of the "democracy" party, however, saw things differently. The local government wanted to expedite a "public assurance" of welcome to the President-elect,[59] and include blaring drums and trumpets, roar of artillery and "other noise and bustle."[60] The Jackson Men planned to meet him in Georgetown and accompany him to his hotel "preceded by a marching band and the appropriate firing of cannon…[61]" Most of these plans went astray, however, as Tennessee Senator John Eaton, knowing Jackson was in the vicinity of Washington, rode out in a plain carriage pulled by two horses to Rockville to bring the Old General into town, leaving the remainder of his party to follow behind him several hours later. Presumably, this tactic would allow Jackson to go on into Washington essentially un-bothered by great crowds of people. By the time Eaton's carriage got to Georgetown, the Central Committee had caught on, met him on horseback and escorted him to Gadsby's Hotel.[62] He arrived at this famous lodging house about 10 a.m., catching most of his friends in the capital unawares; by 2 p.m., however, word had gotten around and cannon salutes thundered from several points in the city.[63]

The two riders, Robert Hays and Andrew Jackson, Jr., whom the President-elect had sent ahead when they passed through Brownsville, Pennsylvania, had arrived in Washington on February 6th. Among other things, they inspected presidential lodgings,[64] which, in fact, had been arranged for Jackson several weeks earlier. He was to stay at John Gadsby's hotel, generally known as The National, on the corner of 6th Street and Pennsylvania Avenue.

A two-roomed parlor was next to two "drawing," or sitting, rooms, both of which could be used at the same time for any large audiences that might arrive.[65] The parlor overlooked a terrace "where he may be saluted from the avenue (Pennsylvania Avenue) by any number of the people who will throng to gaze on their favorite."[66]

And, of course, the large crowds came, as was fully expected. During the first week or so of his stay at the National Hotel, Jackson set aside three hours each day—from noon to 3 p.m.— to meet common, ordinary citizens; after all, he was going to be the "People's President."[67] So many citizens took him up on this offer to meet and talk with the next president that his rooms at the National, or Gadsby's, were nicknamed "The Wigwam."[68] Not too long after they started, the citizen audiences or "powwows" were discontinued because they physically took too much "out of him and deprived him of valuable time needed for his 'public duties.'"[69] He began to limit himself to meetings with possible appointees to his cabinet and other official departments.

At the very hour Jackson entered Washington, both houses of Congress were preparing to count the presidential electoral votes. Senators and Congressmen gathered in the House of Representatives, and at noon on the 11th—the second Wednesday in February—and with John C. Calhoun presiding (who was re-elected as the Vice-President), the votes from the states' electors were taken.[70] It was already known that Jackson had received 178 electoral votes, but the Senate certification was constitutionally mandated.

Back at the "Wigwam," Jackson and his party waited for a joint committee of the Senate and House to arrive. Virginia Senator LittletonTazewell was its spokesman, and he addressed the President-elect in a prepared statement, which read in part:

"It is my duty to notify you that you have been duly elected President of the United States…[We]…confidently believe that [your presidency]…will benefit our common country…[and show]… the respect and esteem and confidence of your fellow-citizens which have been so fully illustrated in your recent election."[71]

Jackson received this message with "feelings of the deepest sensibility."[72] He accepted the "high trust" conferred on him by his fellow citizens." He was well aware of the "responsibilities which it enjoins," promising to "promote the prosperity and happiness of our country."[73]

This was the moment for which Jackson had been waiting. He had not wanted to arrive in Washington City before he was duly certified by the Senate as the next president; nor had he wanted to come into town several days after this procedure. His arrival on the very day that the electoral votes were counted and certified was not just a happy coincidence; he had planned it that way ever since he left the Hermitage.

For the next twenty-two days, Jackson resided at Gadsby's, working still on his inaugural speech, considering cabinet members and entertaining friends in his presidential suite. He arose early on the morning of March 4th, Inauguration Day. At about 11 a.m. he started out on foot from the Gadsby Hotel. The "central committee" was not going to be put off on this occasion, as it had been when he arrived. With Jackson and his traveling companions walking in the middle of Pennsylvania Avenue and with great crowds on either side with horses prancing, cannons booming and drums beating, there was definitely more noise than the President-elect wanted.

Citizens chosen by the Central Committee to attend to the President-elect as he made his way to the Capitol assembled on the west side of Gadsby's, with the foot "passengers" on the sidewalks and carriages and those on horseback in the Avenue, but taking care not to get ahead of Jackson. Just behind the President-elect marched a large regiment of veterans from the Revolution, and behind these old soldiers the rank and file, "without regard" to "station," brought up the rear.[74] As they approached the Capitol's west entrance, the "foot procession" veered to the north gate; the carriages and horses filed off to the south side of the Capitol building.[75]

The "grand marshal" for these procedures was Colonel Nathan Towson. He and most of the other marshals in the District of Columbia were to make certain that Jackson arrived safely at the Capitol and was escorted to the Senate chambers where he would await the beginning of the swearing-in festivities. The Senate, in session when Jackson entered, postponed further business to welcome the next Chief Executive. Jackson sat in front of the Senate clerk with members of the Supreme Court on his right and foreign ministers from several countries on his left.[76]

Conspicuous by his absence was outgoing President John Quincy Adams. Jackson had not paid a courtesy call on the President when he entered Washington in mid-February. In fact, he was hostile to the President, believing that he had encouraged some of the scurrilous attacks on Rachel during the 1828 presidential race. Interestingly enough, John Quincy Adams' father, John Adams, had shunned Thomas Jefferson's swearing-in ceremonies on March 4, 1801, largely on grounds of vast political differences.

At noon on Wednesday, March 4, 1829, Jackson was led to the Capitol's east portico. He was soon joined by Supreme Court Chief Justice John Marshall, who proceeded to give the Oath of Office. Jackson placed his left hand on a Bible that had been brought from the Hermitage, (probably held in place for him by Emily Donelson), raised his right hand and took the following thirty-five word oath:

"I do solemnly swear that I will faithfully execute the Office of President of the United States, and will to the best of my Ability, preserve, protect and defend the Constitution of the United States." When he had completed this Oath of Office, he was no longer the President-elect.

Andrew Jackson was now the President of the United States.

Locomotive, circa 1837

Chapter 11

COMING HOME
_____

President Jackson rode a spirited horse from the Capitol down Pennsylvania Avenue to his new home, the White House, but could not stay very long. Thousands of citizens, who had been gathering in the capital city for at least the last month waiting for the Old Hero's arrival—some estimates went as high as 20,000—were now partying and celebrating in every room of the structure. What they didn't drink from pre-prepared punch bowls they spilled on the floor, ruining expensive carpets and destroying fine glassware; even doors and windows, with people trying to shove themselves into the building, were damaged or destroyed. Several chairs and sofas collapsed under the weight of dozens of heavy boots.

Jackson proved helpless in this situation, "sinking into a listless state of exhaustion."[1] The entire incident proved to many observers such as Daniel Webster, Henry Clay and former President John Quincy Adams, that Andrew Jackson was not fit to be President. If the events of Jackson's first day in office did not prove that "King Mob" had now taken over the country, nothing would.

Many of those who had traveled with Jackson from the Hermitage shielded him as best they could. They threw an arm-locked cordon around him with their bodies and with effort propelled him to the nearest back-door exit. When they finally got him out onto the lawn, they decided that he could not spend his first night as President in the White House. Escorted by capital policemen back to Gadsby's, he spent the late afternoon and early evening there, finally getting the peace and quiet that he wanted. His traveling party allowed a ball that night, but Old Hickory showed up for only a short time. The next day, he returned to the White House and the mobs were gone.

It was, therefore, only on his second day in the presidential office that Jackson actually began running the affairs of government. For the next eight years (he was re-elected in 1832, defeating his old enemy from Kentucky, Henry Clay) he worked diligently for what he considered to be the welfare of the country. The major activities of his presidency may be summarized:

1. The Eaton Affair. Jackson appointed Tennessee Senator, John Eaton, as his Secretary of War. Eaton had married a woman named Margaret (Peggy) O'Neal Timberlake, whose first husband was a seaman. On one of his long voyages, he was apparently lost at sea. During his absences, a rumor swept through Washington that Peggy and Eaton had an affair and that their marriage to each other was "scandalous."

Jackson defended Peggy because it reminded him of the harsh rumors against his own beloved wife, Rachel. Nevertheless, all of the cabinet wives refused to have anything to do with her. The Eaton Affair or "Eaton Malaria," as some called it, persisted for the better part of a year; finally Jackson asked his entire cabinet to resign. Within the first year of his presidency, then, he had to pick an entirely new cabinet to help him run the government.

2. Internal Improvements. Jackson passed through Maysville, Kentucky on his way to the seat of government. Yet, when a bill came before him to fund money for a road from Maysville to Lexington in Kentucky, Jackson vetoed it. He argued it was completely within the borders of one state, and thus did not qualify to be a part of the National Road. Besides, he was not going to approve anything that Henry Clay wanted. Jackson stated that the only way federally financed internal improvements could be legal was for a Constitutional Amendment to be passed authorizing them. His veto cost him a large number of friends in the rapidly developing western parts of the country.

3. Treatment of Native Americans. Andrew Jackson in his time became widely known as an "Indian fighter." He and his armies had defeated the Creeks at the Battle of Horseshoe Bend in Alabama during the War of 1812. On a personal basis, however, he often befriended Indians. He adopted a young Indian, Lecoyah, who lived with him until Lecoyah's death at age 17.

As President, Jackson believed in a policy known as "Indian Removal." He wanted to force Indians, especially a tribe in

Georgia, the Cherokees, to lands west of the Mississippi River. The Cherokees lived in Georgia and they could not keep the white men from taking over their properties. Despite a Supreme Court decision against it, Jackson began the movement that came to be called "The Trail of Tears," a forced march of thousands of Indians to the territory of Oklahoma. They suffered much hardship on this trek to the West. No American should feel pride about the government's policy toward Native Americans: it was a case of the white man spreading out into territories and the Indians trying to keep them away. Ultimately, the Indians failed.

4. The Bank War. Andrew Jackson disliked banks; he had suffered business setbacks earlier in his life that he blamed on dealings with banks. When he became President, his disdain of banks manifested itself in his battle with the Second Bank of the United States.

The second Bank's charter was to expire in 1836; however, the Whigs, led by Henry Clay and Bank President, Nicholas Biddle, decided to make it a political issue in 1832 by trying to get its charter renewed until 1851. They believed that if Jackson vetoed the re-charter, he would lose votes in the North; if he supported it, he would lose votes in the South. He vetoed it in July, 1832, and it went down in U.S. history as one of the more significant presidential rejections of a congressional action. He claimed that it was "Undemocratic" (because only the wealthiest could buy stock in it); and "UnAmerican," (because too many foreigners owned stock in the Bank, especially the British).

The Bank, the President believed, possessed a monetary monopoly in the United States, and he felt that the government should not support monopolies. His clear intent came to be the total destruction of the bank; it was "not too big to fail," as has been argued in our own time on behalf of some corporations.

5. Nature of the Union. One of the most famous debates in American history occurred during Andrew Jackson's presidency. Robert Hayne of South Carolina and Daniel Webster of Massachusetts debated with each other in the Senate over the nature of the American Union. Was it a loose "confederation," from which a state or states could leave or secede? Or was it a tight

"federation," from which no state would have the right to leave and become independent of the Union?

Everyone wondered about President Jackson's viewpoint. Would he support Hayne, who wanted a "confederation," or Webster, who spoke for a "federation." The suspense was ended on April 13, 1830, at an annual observance of Thomas Jefferson's birthday. Jackson was, of course, invited and he listened carefully to all the toasts given, most in favor of Hayne's "confederation" point of view. When Jackson's turn came, he raised his glass and said: "Our Union—it must be preserved." With these few words, President Jackson made it clear where he stood on the Hayne-Webster debate. The Federal Union was the supreme law of the land and he showed in the future, as he had in the past, that he would defend it.

6. "Executive Supremacy." Who was the only national governmental official who represented the entire country? Andrew Jackson said it was the President. The popularly elected House of Representatives was made up of delegates from congressional districts and the Senate was appointed by State Legislatures. The Supreme Court was appointed: in no sense of the word were the justices elected. The only official, therefore, universally elected to office was the President (and, of course, the Vice-President as well). Should it not stand to reason, therefore, that the President would have more power than the Congress or the Court; that the President should be the chief representative of each and every citizen in the United States?

He used his ideas of "executive supremacy" in several ways. One of the most effective was the veto power, particularly in reference to internal improvements and the Second Bank of the United States. He also used patronage; that is, appointing only those people who would support his presidency, and he was frequently denounced for running a "spoils system," of exclusively naming Democrats to fill government positions.

7. Numerous reforms occurred during the eight years that President Jackson was in the White House. Although not personally responsible for most of them, he supported them through the influences of his office.

Medical improvements included more humane treatment of

mentally ill citizens than previously with a remarkable woman, Dorothea Dix, leading the way in this reform. Also schools for the blind and hearing impaired originated throughout the country. In the area of schooling, public education at tax-payers' expense increasingly became a reality, with numerous educational reformers, of whom Horace Mann of Massachusetts was probably the most significant, constantly reporting on the importance of the educational process. Newly-formed newspapers strongly recommended public education, as did labor unions, and idealistic people argued that a Democracy must have an educated citizenry.

Jackson himself wanted to see U.S. senators elected by the public at large. It was not until the Twentieth Century that this proposal became a reality. The 17th Amendment to the Constitution, put into effect in 1913, provided for the direct election of Senators. He stated on occasions that he wanted the President himself to be popularly elected, which would have meant, of course, the destruction of the Electoral College. Even in the early 21st century, one can still hear arguments against the Electoral College and for a country-wide popular vote to put a President into office.

Many historians refer to Jackson's presidency as "The Age of Jackson," in which "Democracy" became a favored form of government. He was the most assertive president up to that time in our history, and his example encouraged a few other "strong" presidents in the future, such as Abraham Lincoln and the two Roosevelts, Theodore and Franklin, in the 20th century.

The election of 1836 went according to Jackson's wishes. His second vice-president, Martin Van Buren, collected a majority of electoral votes to become the eighth president of the United States. He was inaugurated on March 4, 1837, which fell on a Saturday. In the audience, watching Van Buren take the Oath of Office (administered by newly-appointed Chief Justice, Roger B. Taney) was a proud out-going President, Andrew Jackson. Was he happy to leave the presidential office? In a word YES; he was most anxious to get back to the Hermitage and resume his life as a planter.

Mingling in the crowds just after the inauguration of President Van Buren, Jackson was approached by a friend, who said "I congratulate you, Sir…. I congratulate you on your retirement. You are on this day more fortunate than your successor. You are laying down your cares while he is taking them up."[2] The outgoing president, with "flushed cheeks and eyes sparkling with happiness,"[3] replied, "Yes, you are right, Sir, I am now happy. I lay down my office with delight—I am now free from care."[4] Just the day before, on Friday the 3rd, he had remarked to another friend that, "the mines of Peru would not induce me to remain in this House six months longer."[5] He was obviously obsessed with the thought of getting back to his beloved Hermitage.

If he could have had his way about it, Jackson would have left Washington the second Van Buren lowered his right hand at the end of the Oath of Office. He was ill, however, and many of his friends urged him to wait until his health improved before embarking on another long journey. Of course, "long journeys" had never bothered him greatly in the past; but now he was 69 years old; within a few days (March 15) he would turn 70. The best his successor, Van Buren, could do was convince the Old General to stay at the White House at least through the weekend, if not longer, before heading south. At Jackson's protest, Van Buren ordered the Surgeon General of the United States, Dr. Thomas Lawson, to accompany the ex-President at least as far as Wheeling,[6] and further if necessary. When Jackson voiced his disagreement with this arrangement, Van Buren smilingly told him that the Surgeon General was "under the orders of the President of the United States."[7] This was the kind of language Andrew Jackson understood, and there he let the matter drop.

He took his final leave of Washington on Monday, March 6, 1837.[8] He traveled by coach over to the train depot at Second Street and Pennsylvania Avenue, Northwest,[9] where he boarded an especially outfitted Baltimore and Ohio (B&O) train, headed to Baltimore, where the ex-President wished to call upon Chief Justice Roger Taney (pronounced "Tawny"), whom he had appointed when John Marshall died in 1835.

An observer noted that Jackson sat comfortably in his coach, waiting for the nine a.m. train to start toward Baltimore. A special car was attached to the train that housed his "travelling carriages," and another car housed a few horses that would pull him southward once the railroads ended.

The B&O was the oldest railroad in the country. In fact, Jackson took a ride on it in 1832, the first president ever to ride a train. He went to Baltimore by horse carriage and then rode a train from Baltimore to Ellicott Mills, Maryland. The train cars at that time were little more than old stagecoaches outfitted with railroad wheels. A scant five years later, railroads had made spectacular advances and improvements. The Age of the Steamboat had begun a mere generation before; now the railroads in the 1830s and on into the 1840s indicated that, not only would they overtake coaches and steamboats, but surpass them in a few years. By the end of the 1830s, there were "450 locomotives in the country… and 3,200 miles of track."[10]

Before the train started, Jackson sat "composedly" in his car, smoking one of his long-stemmed pipes[11] with tobacco that had probably been grown at the Hermitage. His traveling companions did likewise, some with cigars, considerably fogging up the train compartment. A reporter called the pipe-smoking "a very bad example… for if followed by others, public conveyances would become intolerable to those not accustomed to the refinement of pipes and cigars."[12] Now and then some bystanders broke through the lines to shake Jackson's hand and to say a few words to him. As the train lurched into movement, Jackson walked to the rear platform and waved to the large crowds who had gathered to see him leave. Biographer Marquis James described Jackson's departure from Washington in colorful terms:

"The conductor rang his bell. With a hiss of steam the cars began to move. General Jackson bowed. The crowd stood still. The train swung around a curve, its course described by a trailing plume of smoke. When this dissolved in the air the crowd began to melt away feeling, one has said, 'as if a bright star had gone out of the sky.'"[13] Jackson had taken many trips back to Tennessee while President, as well as tours of the East Coast and New England, but this one aboard a B&O railroad heading for Baltimore, however, was by far the happiest.

Traveling with the Old General—other than the Surgeon

General—was Andrew Jackson Donelson, Rachel's nephew, and Jackson's private secretary throughout his presidential years. Sadly, Donelson's wife, Emily, who had acted as White House hostess for much of Jackson's terms in office, died on December 19, 1836, from one of the 19th century's greatest medical fears, tuberculosis. Others with Jackson included Speaker of the House of Representatives, James K. Polk (called "Young Hickory" by some because of his closeness to Jackson) and his wife, Sarah; and Andrew Jackson, Jr. (another of Rachel's nephews) and his wife, also named Sarah.

Jackson's friends worried about his health and his condition to travel such a long distance. He still suffered from gastrointestinal problems and had to keep a close watch on his diet. He had not been well during 1836; in fact, one newspaper had spoken of "the brief interval of time which separates him from eternity."[14] Another echoed this thought by writing that "during some part of the winter [1836] he did not expect ever to revisit Tennessee but as a corpse."[15]

A few weeks before his presidency ended, he suffered a hemorrhage from the lungs which "threatened a speedy end to my existence."[16] He recovered in time to attend Van Buren's inauguration, but his friends and well-wishers were still concerned about his health. In addition to all his other difficulties he began to show signs of a malady called dropsy, abnormal accumulations of fluid under the skin or other bodily cavities, a condition that continued to worsen in the months and years ahead.

He spent a pleasant day and a half as the guest of Chief Justice Taney in Baltimore. He rested a great deal during this time and then, on Thursday, March 9, he set out once again—by the B&O Railroad for its western terminus, still at Ellicott Mills, Maryland, some thirty miles from Baltimore. Arriving in Ellicott Mills, aides and assistants went about the tasks of removing the carriages from the cars that stored them as well as releasing the horses from their specially equipped compartments. From Ellicott Mills, the ex-President's cavalcade continued westward, toward Wheeling, Virginia.

President Van Buren's order for Surgeon General Lawson to accompany Jackson at least as far as Wheeling turned out to be well-founded. When they arrived in Frostburg, Maryland, Jackson had another of his "indispositions."[17] His onward journey had to be delayed by a day as Surgeon General Lawson administered to his needs. It is almost for certain that Jackson and his party stayed at Highland Hall Hotel in Frostburg, an establishment that was described in 1837 as "commodious and elegant." This hotel, located on the National Road leading into Frostburg from the east, could accommodate 300 guests and see to the interests of passengers on board the thirty-five to forty stagecoaches that stopped there on a daily basis. (There was another hotel in Frostburg at this time, Sandspring Inn, considerably smaller than Highland Hall, and on the west side of town, making it inconvenient for the travelers; thus, an unlikely place for them to have stayed).

After the unexpected stopover in Frostburg, the traveling party made its way back through Uniontown and Washington (on March 14) in Pennsylvania arriving in Wheeling,[18] Virginia, on March 15—which happened to be his 70th birthday. He ordered that no festivities be planned for this day, because he wanted to wait until he got back home to the Hermitage, before observing his date of birth.[19]

The crowds at Wheeling who turned out to see him were, in fact, larger than the ones he had encountered in 1829 on the way to his inauguration in Washington. Eight years before, most Wheeling citizens had treated him shabbily; now they welcomed him "with the greatest enthusiasm."[20] In all likelihood, they came out, despite the ex-President's wishes, to wish him a happy birthday, with many happy returns. It could also have meant that the good citizens were happy to see him heading away from the capital city, rather than towards it.

After spending the night in Wheeling, he boarded the sidewheeler, Steamboat Fayette on March 16. The Fayette weighing 112 tons, with Captain Kemble commanding, was built at Brownsville, Pennsylvania, with its home base in Pittsburgh. (After taking Jackson home in 1837, the Fayette stayed in service until 1843).

Jackson rode down the Ohio River, non-stop, to Cincinnati. He stopped there briefly and was escorted to the home of an old friend,

General R. T. Lytte, where he stayed for a few hours.[21] When leaving Cincinnati he picked up another friend, Ohio Senator William Allen, who traveled with him on to Nashville.[22] It now seemed that his health improved with each and every mile he traveled toward the South.

The local Democratic Party committee at Louisville chartered a special steamboat to go up the Ohio to meet the ex-President, and accompany him to Kentucky. They found him some forty miles above Cincinnati, where both boats approached Cincinnati "with flags flying" and a band playing "the most enlivening tunes."[23] Jackson arrived in Louisville at 7:30 a.m. on March 20, amid huge demonstrations of affection for him. A "Committee of Arrangements" met him and, in a "splendid" open barouche pulled by four "beautiful grey horses," escorted him to lodgings that had been prepared for him at the Louisville Hotel.[24] Though nearing physical exhaustion, Jackson was "called upon" by hundreds of well wishers. He seemed particularly interested in greeting ladies and small children, "their countenances beaming with affection."[25]

As the Fayette pulled away from the Louisville wharf in the early evening, a band struck up Hail Columbia.[26] Some seventy Louisville "gentlemen" rode with Jackson as far as Portland, some three miles downstream. The boat landed at Portland, where the Louisvillians disembarked. As the Fayette once again departed, great crowds of people on the shore "cheered the general as long as he was in sight, and another band struck up the "melodious" tune of Home Sweet Home.[27]

The Fayette now continued day and night toward the south, non-stop all the way. At Smithland, Kentucky, the travelers reached the confluence of the Ohio and Cumberland Rivers. Not even there, however, did the boat stop or even slow down. Jackson's trip was now upriver, but the mood of everyone on the boat was decidedly upbeat. They came to Nashville late on March 24, and arrived at the Hermitage, amid much rejoicing from friends and neighbors,[28] on Saturday, March 25, 1837. He was home! It was not the same Hermitage as he had last left it. The old Hermitage burned in 1836, and this new, colonnaded one, replaced it.

Jackson spent the next several years rarely venturing far from the

Hermitage. He was a "father figure" for thousands of individuals as he gave social and political advice to local people as well as to those scattered around the country. As he aged, and continued to suffer one malady after another, his thoughts increasingly centered around his own mortality. Apparently, he was not alone in these musings because a well intentioned man, Commodore Jesse Duncan Eliot, wanted to send him an ancient Roman sarcophagus, to be used on Jackson's death. Jackson turned down the offer, remarking that he only wanted to be buried next to his beloved Rachel.[29] Surrounded by his family and "servants," and friends from the surrounding areas, Andrew Jackson died on June 8, 1845. He was 78 years old. He was laid to rest beside Rachel in a little cemetery behind the Hermitage.

Over the next several weeks and months, "sham" funerals were held in some sixteen different cities in the country, commemorating the life of Andrew Jackson.[30] The largest of these observances was in New York City, where Jackson had always had at least a modicum of a following. On June 24, 1845, barely two weeks after his death, some 40,000 people—composed of military, civic, and private organizations—marched in a "funeral" procession through the streets of New York, while ten times that number lined up on the sidewalks to watch.[31]

There was even one town in Connecticut—New Englanders almost always professed an animosity toward the seventh president—Norwich, which hoped to show its respects to the late Chief Executive. The Democratic Committee of Arrangements invited a poet, Park Benjamin, to deliver an oration for Jackson. The Committee did not bother to find out that Benjamin was an anti-Jacksonian. He spoke of Jackson's "imperialism," and "lordly tones," while in the presidential office; a man who asked for "power as a right," to "wield it without restraint."[32] The poet's remarks set off a Whig-Democrat newspaper war in Norwich and numerous other parts of the state.[33]

Possibly the most ornate of all the commemorative "funerals" occurred in Louisville, Kentucky, on the very day Jackson was buried at the Hermitage.[34] A "handsome cortege" proceeded out First Street to a 56-acre area known as "Jacob's Woods."[35] Ben Duke, a

90 year old African-American veteran of the Revolution, drove the carriage, pulled by four large horses. Enclosed in the carriage was a "coffin" which was to be buried. A large crowd gathered in front of a house built by George Keats, brother of the poet John Keats,[36] to hear oratory from numerous speakers of the Democratic Party. When the observances ended, all the participants and spectators dispersed quietly, back to their homes.

And so it was at the Hermitage. Andrew Jackson had made the long journey from the Hermitage to Washington, D.C. and then back again. As he was laid beside Rachel, everyone present was aware that now Jackson had embarked on still one more journey; this one, the longest.

ENDNOTES

Chapter 1, Departure

[1] Stanley F. Horn, *The Hermitage: Home of Old Hickory* (Richmond, VA: Garrett & Massie, 1938), p. 134.

[2] S. G. Heiskell, *Andrew Jackson and Early Tennessee History* (Nashville: Ambrose Printing Company, 1920), p. 453.

[3] Ibid.

[4] Ibid., p. 135.

[5] Augusta (GA) *Chronicle and Georgia Advertiser*, February 2, 1829.

Chapter 2, A Tragic Irony

[1] James McCague, *The Cumberland* (NY: Holt, Rinehart and Winston, 1973), p. 90.

[2] Kathleen Krull and Kathryn Hewitt, *Lives of the Presidents: Fame, Shame (And What the Neighbors Thought)* (NY: Harcourt-Brace, 1998), p. 27. See also Jon Meacham *American Lion: Andrew Jackson in the White House*, (New York: Random House, 2008), p. 22, and Daniel Walker Howe, *What Hath God Wrought: The Transformation of America, 1815-1848*, (New York: Oxford University Press, 2007), p. 277.

[3] James Parton, "Jackson's First Election as President (1828), in Francis W. Halsey, *Great Epochs in American History*, vol vi (New York: Current Literature Publishing Company, 1912), p. 9.

[4] *Upland Union (NY), December 23, 1828.*

[5] *Hagerstown Mail*, (Maryland), February 13, 1829.

[6] Rachel Jackson to Louise Moreau Davezec de Lassy Livingston, December 1, 1828. *The Papers of Andrew Jackson* (Knoxville: The University of Tennessee Press, 1961), pp. 536-37.

[7] The Inn was described as equal in "comfort, convenience, and appearance" as any "hotel in the Western country." Rooms and

apartments for families and ladies were separate from the "public part of the house," so that "ladies can be as private as in any house in the city." The Nashville Inn was also the departure station for all of the coaches leaving the city. It quickly became "The" place to stay when visiting Nashville. *The Banner-Whig*, December 27, 1828.

[8] Horn, p. 155.

[9] Ibid.

[10] *Norwich Republican* (VA.), February 4, 1829.

[11] Ibid. The practice of bleeding went all the way back to the Roman period, when one of its famous physicians, Galen, practiced it. Several places on the body, from head to toe, were identified as the best spots for this procedure. A small incision was made with a scalpel and the blood usually flowed from the patient into a pan or other receptacle. Today, it is known that bleeding, except perhaps for reducing high blood pressure, was largely ineffective in treating ailments.

[12] *Norwich Republican*, February 4, 1829.

[13] Gerald W. Johnson, *Andrew Jackson: An Epic in Homespun* (NY: Minton, Balch & Co., 1927), pp. 233-34.

[14] Ibid.

[15] Horn, *The Hermitage*, p. 155.

[16] Parton, p. 10.

[17] The quotes here are from Horn, *The Hermitage*, p. 157.

[18] Ibid.

[19] *Knoxville Register*, December 31, 1828. Also S. G. Heiskell, *Andrew Jackson and Early Tennessee History, vol 1* (Nashville: Ambrose Printing Co., 1920), p. 188.

[20] Horn, *The Hermitage*, 134.

[21] *Hagerstown Mail*, February 13, 1829.

[22] Nashville *Banner-Whig* December 27, 1828.

[23] Andrew's mother, Elizabeth, always wanted him to become a preacher of the gospel. Rachel, while stopping well before the ministry, got Andrew to stop swearing so much, though he did continue to exclaim "By the Eternal," on things he considered awesome. Not exactly a swear phrase, some religious puritanists did look upon it as quite close to blasphemy.

[24] Quotes are from Pauline Wilcox Burke, *Emily Donelson of*

Tennessee, volume 1 (Richmond, VA:, Garrett and Massie, Inc., 1941), p. 159.

[25] Heiskell, 456.

[26] Ibid.

[27] *New-Hampshire Patriot and State Gazette*, January 26, 1829. He did not go through Philadelphia on his journey, nor did he need to. Also see *American Friend & Marietta (*Ohio*) Gazette*, January 10, 1829.

[28] *New Hampshire Patriot and State Gazette* January 26, 1829.

[29] Ibid.

[30] Ibid.

[31] Horn, 156.

[32] *Hagerstown Mail*, February 13, 1829.

[33] Notice that he said "forget," not "forgive." For the rest of his life he believed that the three main culprits in Rachel's death were John Quincy Adams, John C. Calhoun, and Henry Clay.

[34] Heiskell, pp. 456–457.

[35] *Hagerstown Mail*, February 13, 1829.

[36] James Parton, *Life of Andrew Jackson*, vol 111 (New York: Mason Brothers, 1860), p. 15.

Chapter 3, "An Afflictive Dispensation of Providence"

[1] Letter, Andrew Jackson to Katherine Duane Morgan; January 3, 1829. *Andrew Jackson Papers*, Vol. VII (Knoxville, University of Tennessee Press, 1961), p. 5.

[2] *Vermont Gazette* (Bennington, VT) February 3, 1829, p. 2.

[3] *Richmond* (VA) *Enquirer*, January 29, 1829, p. 3.

[4] *New Hampshire Patriot and State Gazette*, January 19, 1829, p. 3.

[5] *Richmond* (VA) *Enquirer*, January 20, 1829, p. 3.

[6] Ibid.

[7] *United States Telegraph* (Washington, D.C.), January 26, 1829. (Reprinted from the *Louisville Advertiser*, December 19, 1828).

[8] *Argus of Western America*, January 28, 1829. On the same day, January 8, 1829, according to one of Jackson's early biographers, James Parton, a group of individuals in Hartford, Connecticut, (an area that strongly opposed the War of 1812, in which Jackson had been so instrumental), burned the President-elect in effigy. The city

fathers were so outraged by this act that they offered a reward of one hundred dollars for the "conviction of the persons engaged in it." See James Parton, *Life of Andrew Jackson*, Vol. III (NY: Mason Brothers, 1860), p. 166.

[9] *Argus of Western America*, January 28, 1829.

[10] Ibid.

[11] Quoted in Arthur M. Schlesinger, Jr., *The Age of Jackson* (Boston: Little, Brown & Co., 1945), p. 4.

[12] Parton, Vol III, p. 267.

[13] Quoted in William Graham Sumner, *Andrew Jackson* (Boston: Houghton-Mifflin, 1924), p. 179.

[14] Nashville *Banner-Whig*, January 3, 1829.

[15] Ibid.

[16] Ibid.

[17] Ibid.

[18] Ibid.

[19] William Story (ed), *Life and Letters of Joseph Story*, Vol 1 (Freeport, NY: Books for Libraries Press, 1971), p. 562.

[20] Mary C. Francis, *A Son of Destiny: The Story of Andrew Jackson* (New York: The Federal Book Company, 1902), p. 165.

[21] *Norwich Republican*, February 4, 1829, p. 74.

[22] The author is indebted to Russ Lampkins of Ingram Barge Company in Paducah, Kentucky, for these mileages. One must remember that the Cumberland and Ohio Rivers had twists and turns and even "flowbacks" that made travel on them longer than by land. For example from Cincinnati to Wheeling is some 250 miles by land; nearly 400 by the Ohio River.

[23] Jackson to Richard Call, December 22, 1828. *The Jackson Papers* (Knoxville: The University of Tennessee Press, 1961, V. VII), pp. 546-547.

[24] Ibid.

[25] Ibid.

[26] Glen Vecchione, *The Little Giant Book of American Presidents* (NY: Sterling, 2007), pp. 20-21. Consult also William DeGregario, *Complete Book of U.S. Presidents*; Christine Putnam, *But the President Wants Meat Loaf*, and Judy Asman, *Favorite Foods of U.S. Presidents.*

[27] See Diane Heilenman, "Boys of Bourbon: The Lore Behind the Labels," in *The Courier-Journal* (Louisville, KY), May 3, 2009.

[28] James MacGregor Burns and Susan Dunn, *George Washington* (NY: Times Books, 2004), p. 3.

[29] Letter, Lyman Beecher to Ezra Stiles Ely; January 20, 1829. Quoted in John Spencer Bassett, *Correspondence of Andrew Jackson* (Washington, D.C.: Carnegie Institute of Washington, 1902), p. 3.

[30] Ibid.

[31] Ezra Stiles Ely to Andrew Jackson; January 28, 1829. Quoted in John Spencer Bassett, *Correspondence of Andrew Jackson* (Washington, D.C.: Carnegie Institute of Washington, 1902), p. 3.

[32] Ibid.

[33] Ibid.

[34] Ibid.

[35] Letter, Charles Coffin to Andrew Jackson, January 21, 1829. *The Papers of Andrew Jackson, v vii* (Knoxville: The University of Tennessee Press, 2007), p. 16.

[36] Ibid. The 27th Verse of Jeremiah 17, seems to have been the Reverend's main point of emphasis. "... If ye will not hearken unto me to hallow the sabbath day... then I will kindle a fire... and it shall devour the palaces of Jerusalem, and it shall not be quenched." King James Version of the Bible, p. 717.

[37] Ibid. The quote is from Verse 25. Also Coffin letter to Jackson, January 21, 1829. *Papers of Andrew Jackson, v ii* (Knoxville: University of Tennessee Press, 2007), p. 17.

[38] "Gen. Jackson: Washington; Sunday; Providence; Mr. Adams." *Connecticut Mirror*, February 14, 1829, p. 3.

[39] Ibid.

[40] Ibid.

[41] Ibid

[42] Ibid.

Chapter 4, On the River

[1] Story, vol. II, p. 21.

[2] Ibid., p. 25.

[3] Ibid.

[4] See Booth Tarkington, *The Magnificent Ambersons* (Gloucester, Mass: Peter Smith, 1967), p. 48.

[5] John H. White, Jr. *Steamboats on the Inland Rivers* (Oxford, Ohio: The Walter Havingshurst Special Collections," n.d.), pp. 2-21.

[6] Byrd Douglas, *Steamboatin' on the Cumberland* (Nashville: Tennessee Book Company, 1961), p. 2.

[7] James McCaque, *The Cumberland* (New York: Holt, Rinehart & Winston, 1973), p. xiii.

[8] Ibid.

[9] Douglas, *Steamboatin'*, p. 21.

[10] Ibid.

[11] The rail systems in the 1830s and beyond greatly decreased passenger travel on steamboats and, at least in the East, stage coach passenger travel. The latter, however, became the major means of passenger transportation for the Western settlements.

[12] Alfred Pirtle Collection; Filson Club, Louisville, Kentucky.

[13] Ibid.

[14] John H. White, Jr., *Steamboats on the Inland Rivers* (Oxford, Ohio: The Walter Havinghurst Special Collections, n.d), pp. 12-13.

[15] Robert V. Remini *Andrew Jackson and the Course of American Freedom 1822-1832* (New York: Harper, 1981), p. 158-159.

[16] Moser,"Andrew Jackson, 1767-1845," *The Tennessee Encyclopedia of History and Culture* (Knoxville, University of Tennessee Press, 2002). encyclopedia.net/imagegalley.php?Entry id=J005.

[17] Douglas, *Steamboatin' on the Cumberland*, pp. 22-23.

[18] *Eastern Argus* (Portland, Maine); February 10, 1829.

[19] *The Mountaineer*, (Greenville, SC); February 7, 1829.

[20] *Eastern Argus* (Portland, Maine); February 3, 1829.

[21] White, *Steamboats on the Inland Rivers*, p. 5.

[22] Ibid.

[23] Douglas, *Steamboatin' on the Cumberland*, p. 23.

[24] Horn, *The Hermitage: Home of Old Hickory*, p. 135.

[25] Ibid.

[26] Pauline Wilcox Burke, *Emily Donelson of Tennessee*, (Richmond: Garret and Massie, 1941), p. 175.

[27] This story is recounted in Burke, *Emily Donelson of Tennessee*, pp. 175-76.

[28] *Rhode-Island American and Providence Gazette*, February 10, 1829.

Chapter 5, Further on the River

[1] The author is indebted to Glen Connor, Kentucky state climatologist for this weather information.

[2] Frances Trollope, *Domestic Manners of the Americans*, edited by Donald Smalley (New York: Knopf, 1949), pp. 298-299.

[3] Philo A. Goodwin, *Biography of Andrew Jackson, President of the United States* (New York: R. Hart Towner, 1833), p. 316.

[4] A polyglot bible was one of many different languages. These bibles on board the *Fairy* and other river-boats were undoubtedly intended for the numerous tribes of Indians along the stretches of the Cumberland and the Ohio.

[5] Ursula Smith Beach, *Along the Warioto, or a History of Montgomery County, Tennessee* (Clarksville: Kiwanis Club and Tennessee Historical Commision, 1964), p. 116.

[6] John H. White, *Steamboats on the Inland Rivers* (Oxford, Ohio: The Walter Havinghurst Special Collections, n.d.), p. 15.

[7] For additional descriptions of what Andrew Jackson, his entourage, and fellow passengers saw on the way to Clarksville, consult Beach, *Along the Warioto*, p. viii.

[8] ID=C175.

[9] Byrd Douglas, *Steamboatin' on the Cumberland*, p. 9.

[10] Ibid., p. 10.

[11] Ibid.

[12] Ibid., p. 28. Of course, the most formidable Shoals of them all was Muscle Shoals in Northern Alabama, near the city of Florence, and on the Tennessee River. These shoals made it difficult, if not impossible, to take goods coming up from the South on over to Knoxville, Tennessee. The Harpeth problem was solved nearly a hundred years after Jackson's passage, in 1904, Lock A at Fox's Bluff was constructed. Douglas, p. 10. Through this mechanism, the depth of the water could be manually controlled.

[13] *Cincinnati Daily Gazette*, October 21, 1828.

[14] Ibid. Apparently, Shoemaker's loo was a gambling game with cards in which each player "anted" up a pot, and then played, either with three cards or five cards to win with the highest hands— somewhat similar to today's poker games of "five card" stud or "seven card" stud, or modern whist. James Fenimore Cooper mentioned Shoemaker's Loo on pages 345-346 in his novel, *Home As Found*, in a derogatory sense. People of "high class," for example, would "repair" to some secret room in a tavern where, after carefully locking the door and drawing the curtains, they would "pass a refreshing hour in endeavoring to relieve each other of carrying their odd sixpences by means of a little shoemaker's loo." Outside the taverns and grog shops, however, these "worthies" almost always exhorted their sons and daughters to avoid card games, because they were "sinful." See James Fenimore Cooper, *Home As Found* (New York: The Co-Operative Publication Society, 1884), pp. 345-346. There were limited "loos" and unlimited "loos." The latter caused a great deal of noise and very frequently, violence between and among the players. If a player could not take a "trick"—that is, at least one winning combination of cards in a particular round of play, he had to "loo" by paying a certain sum to the pool; if the game was unlimited, sometimes the "loo" pot could grow to enormous proportions, and rowdy reactions from both players and spectators. "Loo" was a nonsense word in several languages: "lelala," French; "ladidah," English, and several others. How the U.S. version of the game of "loo" came to be called in some instances, "Shoemaker Loo" remains obscure.

[15] S.G. Heiskell, *Andrew Jackson and Early Tennessee History*, vol. 1 (Nashville: Ambrose Printing Company, 1920), p. 413.

[16] *Cincinnati Advertiser,* March 4, 1829; and February 11, 1829.

[17] Ibid.

[18] *Cincinnati Advertiser*, February 11, 1829.

[19] Ralph Earle, presidential painter, lived at the Hermitage for a while as he painted likenesses of Andrew Jackson. Later, he moved to the White House while Jackson was President, and had his own apartments there for a while.

[20] *Cincinnati Advertiser*, February 11, 1829.

[21] Pirtle Papers, (B1 F4896 115) Filson Society, Louisville, Kentucky.

[22] The National Republicans ran Henry Clay for president in 1832, opposing Jackson. The term "Whig" came into general usage in the United States as an anti-Jackson party in 1834. In the election of 1828, Jackson garnered 44,293 popular votes and all eleven of Tennessee's electoral vote. After all, he was definitely considered to be a "native son."

[23] Beach, *Along the Warioto....*," p. 75.

[24] Ibid.

[25] Douglas, *Steamboatin' on the Cumberland,*, p. 26. It was in Kuttawa later that William Kelly invented an "air-boiling" process in steelmaking that later was called "The Bessemer Process."See Douglas, *Steamboatin' on the Cumberland*, p. 26.

[26] Ibid.

Chapter 6, Auld Lang Syne

[1] There is a marker in the Andrew Jackson State Park in the Waxhaws area to indicate Jackson's birthplace. It is known in South Carolina as the "Crawford Cabin."

[2] Article, *Crawford-Hutchinson* (Smithland: Livingston County, KY. Historical Society). n.p.

[3] Jon Meacham, *American Lion: Andrew Jackson in the White House.* (New York: Random House, 2008), p. 10.

[4] Jimmy Phillips "My Connection to the 7th President of the United States," Pamphlet, n.d. Livingston (KY) County Historical Society; Smithland, Kentucky. Phillips (Jane Hutchinson Crawford was his sixth paternal great grandmother) quipped in this article: "I am often asked if I get special treatment due to my connection to Andrew Jackson. And the answer is yes. I am able to get into just about anywhere I want by simply showing a picture of my cousin, as long as it's over a twenty dollar bill." Of course, Jackson's picture is on the $20 bill.

[5] Ibid.

[6] Today, (2011) there is a sign in front of the Gower House (long closed) that names several celebrities and dignitaries who have stayed there. Included are James K. Polk, Zachary Taylor, and Ned

Buntline, a well known author of the time, as well as internationally renowned English writer, Charles Dickens, and Red Cross founder, Clara Barton. Andrew Jackson's name is not listed in this historical marker, presumably because he did not stay overnight; just for several hours on the morning of Tuesday, January 20, 1829. Besides, at the time Jackson visited this establishment, it was known as Bell Tavern, not the Gower House.

[7] Carrie Ann Berryman, *Folklore and Historic Research Concerining the Gower House,* (Paper, Murray State University, 1997), p. 2.

[8] Tracy Cothron, "Smithland; Through the Windows of the Gower House." (Unpublished, undated paper; Livingston Historical Society, Smithland, KY), p. 2.

[9] Ibid., p. 8.

[10] Ibid., pp 2, 9.

[11] Ibid., p. 6.

[12] Ibid., p. 3.

[13] Ibid.

[14] In 1829 Smithland was a real river town. However, just 30 years later, the railroads were overpowering steamboat runs. Railroads could carry more freight than boats, and this is what put Smithland into historical obscurity. Today, Smithland still has a thriving interest in its past, and its "glory days" of steamboat travel.

[15] Cothron, p. 1.

[16] J.A. Caldwell, *History of Belmont and Jefferson Counties* (Wheeling, WVA: The Historical Society), p. 2.

[17] Filson Club Lectures, Alfred Pirtle Collection; B 1 F489b, 05. Filson Club; Louisville, Kentucky.

[18] Ibid.

[19] Ibid.

[20] Samuel Cummings, *The Western Pilot (Cincinnati: Sy N. And Gulford, 1833),* p. 49.

[21] Ibid.

[22] *American Memory;* Library of Congress, Washington, D.C.

[23] Ibid.

[24] *Shawneetown Gazette,* January 24, 1829. This story was re-printed in the *Arkansas Gazette,* February 10, 1829.

Chapter 7, On to the North

[1] The author is indebted to WKU Professor Glen Connor, State Climatologist for Kentucky, for supplying temperature and weather information for this study.

[2] John Sharkey Papers, A S 5 31; Filson Club; Louisville, Kentucky.

[3] Ibid.

[4] He had begun writing his inaugural address at the home of his friend, William Lewis, before his journey. Both Lewis and Henry Lee helped him to get started. He used much of his time on board the *Fairy* to put what he hoped would be finishing touches. See James Parton, *Life of Andrew Jackson*, vol 111 (New York: Mason Brothers, 1860), p. 15. He was, however, revising the inaugural speech right up until the time he delivered it on March 4, 1829.

[5] Letter, Jackson to James Ronaldson, Jan. 4, 1829. *Papers of Andrew Jackson, v VII* (Knoxville: University of Tennessee Press, 2007), p. 6.

[6] Sharkey Papers, Filson Club; Louisville, Kentucky.

[7] One story that made the rounds concerned the steamboat *General Jackson* at a time after the inaugural trip of 1829. It seems that the *General Jackson* came up the Louisville and Portland Canal with a bust of the General on the bow. It met another boat coming down the canal, and the Captain of that boat demanded that the Jackson back out and let it pass. The Captain of the *General Jackson* said, "The General doesn't back up for anything." The Captain then directed the deck crew to take the bust of the General and carry it up the canal path to Louisville, while the dispute between the two captains continued. The author is indebted to Chuck Parrish, of Louisville, for this story.

[8] These descriptions come from John Sharkey in the John Sharkey Papers, A S 531; Filson Club; Louisville, Kentucky.

[9] Ibid.

[10] Ibid.

[11] Ironically, just one year into office, Andrew Jackson "pocket" vetoed a bill that would have given federal help to the Portland Canal "for boats to bypass the falls of the Ohio." He considered that such largesse would serve private rather than public interests.

See Carlton Jackson, *Presidential Vetoes, 1792-1945* (Athens: The University of Georgia Press), pp 25-26. But, perhaps, he remembered his trek up from the west side of the river to the east?

[12] These descriptions come from John Sharkey in the John Sharkey Papers, A S 531; Filson Club; Louisville, Kentucky.

[13] George H. Yater, *Two Hundred Years At the Falls of the Ohio: A History of Louisville and Jefferson County* (Louisville: The Heritage Corporation of Louisville and Jefferson County, 1979), p. 31.

[14] John E. Kleber, et al (eds) *The Encyclopedia of Louisville* (Lexington: The University Press of Kentucky, 2001), 404.

[15] Yater, *Two Hundred....,* p. 31.

[16] Ibid.

[17] *Louisville Public Advertiser,* January 24, 1829.

[18] The *Scioto Gazette* (Ohio), February 4, 1829.

[19] Pauline Wilcox Burke, *Emily Donelson of Tennessee,* vol. 1 (Richmond, VA: Garrett and Massie, 1941), p. 164.

[20] Connor Weather Statistics.

[21] *Louisville Public Advertiser,* January 24, 1829.

[22] Merchant Steam Vessels of the United States, 1790-1868 (Providence, Rhode Island: Steamship Society, 2009), p. 170.

[23] *Connecticut Herald,* February 10, 1829.

[24] Remini, *Andrew Jackson...* p. 158.

[25] The story of the Augean Stables is, of course, widely mentioned on the Internet. For a succinct explanation, see the compact Oxford English Dictionary, 2nd ed (Oxford: Clarendon Press, 1989), p. 87.

[26] Stories about the *Hercules* appeared in several newspapers, such as the *Louisville Public Advertiser,* February 7, 1829; *Baltimore Patriot,* February 3, 1829; *Maryland Gazette* (Annapolis, MD), February 5, 1829; and the *Hagerstown Mail* (MD), February 6, 1829.

[27] John Sharkey, *Travel Diary,* July 16-29, 1829. A S 531. Filson Club; Louisville, Kentucky.

[28] Samuel Cummings, *The Western Pilot* (Cincinnati: Sy N. And Guilford, 1833), p. 49.

[29] Ibid., p. 45.

Chapter 8, Cincinnati

[1] W.T. Coggeshall, *The Poets and Poetry of the West* (Columbus, OH: Follett, Foster & Co, 1860), p ?1.

[2] Henry Clay to Norbert Beall, nd, 1829. Beall-Booth Family Letters, A B 365; 52.66.68; Filson club; Louisville, Kentucky. The phrase, "looker on in Venice," was used quite frequently in the nineteenth century to mean some kind of neutrality; that one would stand on the "side-lines," and not be central to any decision-making processes. Of course, while Jackson was in office (1829-1837) Henry Clay did everything except maintain any kind of neutrality toward the seventh president.

[3] Aaron Burr, Vice President under Thomas Jefferson, was accused of conspiring with Spanish authorities to detach portions of American territory from the United States and give them to Spain. He visited Jackson at the Hermitage. There is no proof that Jackson had anything to do with the "conspiracy."

[4] This was a reference to a duel between Jackson and Charles Dickinson over various matters, including insults to Rachel. The duel was fought across the state line, in Kentucky, where dueling was legal. Jackson killed Dickinson in this duel.

[5] *Cincinnati Gazette*, August 29, 1828.

[6] Ibid.

[7] *Cincinnati Gazette* October 15, 1828.

[8] *Cincinnati Gazette*, October 21, 1828.

[9] *The New York Commercial*, November 1, 1828.

[10] These quotations are excerpted from the literature of the day.

[11] *Hagerstown* (Maryland) *Mail*, February 13, 1829.

[12] Ibid.

[13] Letter, Robert Punshon to Andrew Jackson, February 6, 1829; *The Papers of Andrew Jackson*, v. vii, 1829. (Knoxville: University of Tennessee Press, 2007), p. 27.

[14] R. Douglas Hurt, *The Ohio Frontier: Crucible of the Old Northwest, 1720-1830* (Bloomington: Indiana University Press, 1998), p. 370.

[15] John Sharkey, *Travel Diary, July 16-29, 1829* ; Filson Club, A S 5 3 1; Louisville, Kentucky.

[16] Hurt, *Ohio Frontier*, p. 370.

[17] Ibid.

[18] Cincinnati *Chronicle*, March 14, 1829.

[19] Ibid.

[20] *The Cincinnati Chronicle*, January 31, 1829.

[21] In the 1790s, John Adams, second President of the United States, had a smallpox vaccination. With his lancet the physician "divided the skin about a quarter of an inch, and just suffering the blood to appear, buried a thread (infected) about a quarter of an inch long in the channel. A little lint was then laid over the scratch and a piece of rag pressed on, and then a bandage bound over all…" When the inoculation took effect, Adams was "confined to hospital for three weeks… with headaches, backaches, knee aches, gagging fever, and eruption of pock marks." See John R. Bumgarner, *The Health of the Presidents: The 41 United States Presidents Through 1993 From a Physician's Point of View* (Jefferson, North Carolina: McFarland, 1994), pp. 9-10.

[22] See Robley Dunglison, *A Dictionary of American Science* 11th ed (Philadelphia: Blanchard and Lea, 1854),

[23] Cummings, *Western Pilot*, p. 41.

[24] Ibid.

[25] Sharkey, *Travel Diary*.

[26] Ibid.

[27] Ibid.

[28] Frances Trollope, *Domestic Manners of the Americans*, David Smalley, ed (New York: Knopf, 1949), pp. xix, xx.

[29] Ibid., p. 142.

[30] Ibid., p. 143.

[31] *New Hampshire Gazette*, February 10, 1829.

[32] *Louisville* (KY) *Advertiser*, February 7, 1829.

[33] Ibid.

[34] Trollope, *Domestic Manners…*, p. 143.

[35] Ibid.

[36] *Cadet and Statesman* (Providence, Rhode Island), February 7, 1829.

[37] Trollope, *Domestic Manners…*, p. 143.

[38] Ibid.

[39] *Louisville* (KY) *Advertiser*, February 7, 1829.

[40] Trollope, *Domestic Manners...*, *p. 145*. See also Robert Remini, *Andrew Jackson...*, p. 156.

[41] Ibid.

[42] Jackson was not only a sharp-shooter with a pistol and rifle, he was also efficient at the use of his heavy cane. In 1835, as he was serving his sixth year in office, an unemployed house painter named Richard Lawrence tried to assassinate him. Fortunately, both of Lawrence's guns misfired, but the infuriated president physically attacked him, and would have seriously injured him, or worse, had not various congressmen and cabinet members pulled him away. See Carlton Jackson, "Another Place, Another Time: The Attempted Assassination of Andrew Jackson," *Tennessee Historical Quarterly*, 26 (Summer, 1967), pp. 184-190.

[43] Trollope, *Domestic Manners...*, p. 145.

[44] *New Hampshire Gazette*, February 10, 1829.

[45] Mark R. Cheathem, *Old Hickory's Nephew: The Political and Private Struggles of Andrew Jackson Donelson* (Baton Rouge: LSU Press, 207), p. 58.

[46] Ibid., p. 54.

Chapter 9, The End of the River

[1] United States National Weather Service: Weather Bureau, 1825-1979.

[2] Ibid.

[3] Weather Notes, Glen Connor, WKU.

[4] Unfortunately for Captain Kierstedt and his colleagues in 1829, Samuel Cummings' book, *The Western Pilot* would not be published for another four years (in 1833). Nevertheless, seasoned steamboat captains knew most of the pitfalls of the Ohio River and piloted their boats accordingly. Cummings work was a detailed description of sandbars, islands and islets in the river, and the best currents available. See Samuel Cummings, *The Western Pilot*, (Cincinnati: SYN and Guilford), 1833.

[5] *Hartford* (Connecticut) *Times*, February 16, 1829.

[6] Cummings, *The Western Pilot*, p. 35.

[7] Sharkey Diary, 1829.

[8] *Hartford Times*, February 16, 1829.

[9] Ibid.

[10] Ibid.

[11] *Hartford Times*, February 16, 1829.

[12] Ibid.

[13] Ibid.

[14] Ibid. Psalms 126 is listed in the Bible as a "song of degrees." The "Songs of Degrees," said one scholar, or "songs of Ascents," are "meant to teach us about our upward journey toward what God wills for His church.

http://www.ronaldridleyministries.com/sermons/page/audio/songpart l. htm

[15] Pauline Wilcox Burke, *Emily Donelson of Tennessee* , v 1 (Richmond: Garrett and Massie Incorporated), p. 164.

[16] Samuel Cummings, *The Western Pilot...*" p. 17.

[17] Ibid.

[18] See George Fetherling, *Wheeling: A Short History* (Wheeling: Polyhedron Learning Media, Inc., 2008), p. 1.

[19] For his services on behalf of the Americans, Ebenezer Zane received several "military warrants," enabling him to select thousands of acres of land for his use. One of the tracts he chose became Zanesville, Ohio, where, on January 30, 1872, his great-great grandson, Zane Grey, was born. Grey became one of the best known authors, particularly of Westerns, in the United States. See Carlton Jackson, *Zane Grey* (Boston: Twayne Publishers, 1973), p. 18.

[20] George Fetherling, Email to the author, January 25, 2009.

[21] *Virginia Statesman*, January 28, 1829.

[22] *Wheeling Gazette*, January 31, 1829.

[23] Josephine Jefferson, *Wheeling Glass* (Mt. Vernon, Ohio: Guide Publications, 1947), p. 27.

[24] Ibid., pp 28-29.

[25] The Jackson flask is still on display at the Oglebay Mansion Museum in Wheeling. It is identified as having been blown to commemorate Old Hickory's stopover in Wheeling in 1829 on his way to Washington to take over the reins of government. George Fetherling, Email to the author; January 25, 2009.

[26] *United State Telegraph*, February 2, 1829.

[27] Ibid.

[28] Ibid.

[29] Ibid.

[30] This animosity toward Andrew Jackson apparently became one of long-standing. In the mid-twentieth century, a Wheeling bank sponsored a short book about Wheeling's history. While this book mentioned visits by the Marquis de Lafayette, Henry Clay, Daniel Webster, and other dignitaries, not a word was given about Jackson's visit in 1829. In fact, his name was not mentioned in any capacity in this book, either as President-elect or as President. Perhaps some of these omissions were due to Jackson's famous (or infamous) veto of the Bank of the United States in 1832, leading to a "bank war" that pitted banks against the President. See *Wheeling's First 250 Years: A Short History done in Celebration of Service to Our Neighbors in Wheeling for half of that Period, 1817-1942* (Wheeling: The National Bank of West Virginia, 1942).

[31] One newspaper at least—the *United States Telegraph*, named the hotel where Jackson stayed in Pittsburgh The Ramsay. *United States Telegraph*, quoting from the *Pittsburgh Mercury*, February 9, 1829. All other sources, however, said it was the Mansion House.

[32] *Cincinnati Daily Gazette*, February 3, 1829.

[33] *United States Telegraph*, quoting from the *Pittsburgh Mercury*, February 9, 1829.

[34] Ibid.

[35] Robert V. Remini, *Andrew Jackson and the Course of American Freedom, 1822-1832* (NY: Harper, 1981), p. 158.

[36] Ibid.

[37] *United States Telegraph*, quoting from the *Pittsburgh Mercury*, February 9, 1829. Some members of this committee were General R. T. Stewart, Henry Baldwin, John McDonald, Patrick Mulvany, Samuel Jones, B. Blackwell, Aaron Hart, and James Eakin—all prominent citizens of Pittsburgh.

[38] Ibid.

[39] *American Friend and Marietta Gazette* (Marietta, Ohio), February 21, 1829.

[40] This article was reprinted in full by the *American Friend & Marietta Gazette* (Marietta, Ohio), February 21, 1829.

[41] Ibid.

[42] Ibid.

[43] *Hagerstown Mail* (Maryland) February 13, 1829.

[44] Which now consisted of Major W.B. Lewis, Captain Donelson and Emily, Mr. Hayes (one of Jackson's adopted sons), Miss Eaton, Mrs. Love and daughter, and Major Lee and his wife. A great many of the women in the group had either been related to Rachel or had been her close friends. They felt, therefore, justified in accompanying the President-elect to Washington City.

[45] *The Pittsburgh Mercury*, quoted in *United States Telegraph*, February 9, 1829.

Chapter 10, Mr. President

[1] See the *Vermont Patriot and State Gazette* (Montpelier); February 9, 1829.

[2] Ibid.

[3] *Baltimore Gazette and Daily Advertiser*, January 30, 1829.

[4] See the *Norwich Courier*, (Norwich, CN), February 4, 1829.

[5] See *Farmer's Cabinet* (Amherst, NH), February 7, 1829.

[6] *Carolina Observer* (Fayetteville, North Carolina), February 5, 1829.

[7] This concern was seen to in February, 1933, when the Twentieth Amendment to the U.S. Constitution was ratified. It states that "If, at the time fixed for the beginning of the term of the President, the President-elect shall have died, the Vice-President-elect shall become President." In 1829, the Twentieth Amendment was still a hundred years away, a situation that led to huge amounts of speculation about who would take the presidential oath on March 4, 1829.

[8] *Portland Advertiser and Gazette of Maine* (Portland, Me), February 2, 1829.

[9] *Farmers' Cabinet* (Amherst, NH), January 28, 1829.

[10] *Augusta Chronicle and Georgia Advertiser* (Augusta, GA), February 11, 1829.

[11] Ibid.

[12] See *Salem Gazette* (Salem, MA), March 2, 1829.

[13] *Farmers' Cabinet* (Amherst, NH), January 28, 1829. Some newspapers which regularly reported on this divisive question

included *Augusta Chronicle* (Augusta, GA), February 4, 1829, February 11, 1929;*Carolina Observer* (Fayetteville, NC), February 5, 1829; *Baltimore Gazette and Daily Advertiser* (Baltimore, MD), January 30, 1829, February 5, 1829; *Baltimore Patriot* (Baltimore, MD), January 29, 1829, February 4, 1829; *Richmond Enquirer* (Richmond, VA), January 29, 1829 February 3, 1829; *Cadet and Statesman* (Providence, RI), February 2, 1829; *Portland Advertiser* (Portland, ME), February 6, 1829; *Salem Gazette*(Salem,MA), February 3, 1829;*Farmers' Cabinet* (Amherst, NH), February 7, 1829; *American Repertory* (St. Albans, PA), January 29, 1829; *Sentinel and Witness* (Middletown, CT), February 11, 1829; and numerous others.

[14] Nowadays this road is Interstate 79 and State Road 19.

[15] *American Friend and Marietta Gazette* (Marietta, Ohio); February 21, 1829.

[16] Home Page, Century Inn. Other famous guests included George Washington, the Marquis de Lafayette, and James K. Polk. The Century Inn has been in continual existence and operation since its first opening in 1794. The author is indebted to Jill Godlewski of the Washington, Pennsylvania, Public Library for this information.

[17] The author is indebted to Ms. Megin Harrington, manager of Century Inn, for this information about the foods that were probably served to Andrew Jackson and his traveling party.

[18] *Aurora & Pennsylvania Gazette* (Philadelphia, PA); February 10, 1829.

[19] Glenn Connor Weather Notes.

[20] Karl Raitz (ed.) *The National Road* (Baltimore: The Johns Hopkins Press, 1996), p. xi. See also *Wheeling's First 250 Years....* p. 19.

[21] *Cincinnati Chronicle,* January 18, 1829.

[22] *Daily Gazette,* January 13, 1829.

[23] *Banner-Whig* (Nashville, Tennessee), December 27, 1828. See also *Cincinnati Gazette*, February 11, 1829.

[24] Seymour Dunbar, *History of Travel*, v. II (Indianapolis: Bobbs-Merrill, 1915), p. 737.

[25] Raitz, *The National Road*, p. 97.

[26] The author is grateful to Mr. Paul Byrd of Brownsville, PA, for this information.

[27] *The Daily News Standard* (Uniontown, PA), November 21, 1930. This newspaper did not authenticate any sources for this story; it could very well have been apochryphal.

[28] Ibid.

[29] The committee members who called on Jackson at the Gibson Inn were Robert Henry, P. Gacsey, Robert Patterson, John Blyth, and N. Iseller. This information was gathered from a letter to the author from Paul E. Byrd, Brownsville Lodge No. 60. The author expresses his thanks.

[30] Minutes of Lodge Number Sixty; Brownsville, Pennsylvania; February 2, 1829, James Fitzsimmons, Secretary.

[31] The electoral counts of each state are cast in each state's capital about a month after the November elections. If the majority of the popular vote goes for a certain candidate, that candidate should win all that state's electoral votes. Then each state sends the results to the Senate which, in the presence of the House of Representatives, certifies these state electoral returns and announces who the next president will be.

[32] *Louisville Public Advertiser* (Louisville, KY); January 21, 1829.

[33] Raitz, *The National Road*, p. 97.

[34] Ibid.

[35] *Richmond Enquirer*, February 10 , 1829.

[36] *The Genius* (Union Town, PA), February 4, 1829.

[37] Ibid.

[38] Connor weather statistics.

[39] Pauline Wilcox Burke, *Emily Donelson of Tennessee* (Richmond, VA: Garrett and Massie, 1941), p. 165.

[40] The cold weather of the 4th gave way to a continuing moderation the next day. By the 6th and 7th of February, temperatures had considerably warmed up, well into the mid-40's. By the time they reached Hagerstown, on Sunday, the 8th, it was raining but still in the comfort zones of 45 degrees. Connor weather statistics.

[41] *Baltimore Patriot* , February 10, 1829.

[42] Thomas J.C. Williams, *History of Washington County, Maryland From the Earliest Settlements to the Present Time*, v 1 (Clearfield Company and Family Line Publications, 1992), p. 186.

[43] Ibid.

[44] *The New York Times*, Obituary for General Henry Kyd Douglas; December 27, 1903.

[45] Ruben Musey, *It happened in Washington County* (Hagerstown: Washington County Bicentennial Committee, 1976), p. 55.

[46] Ibid.

[47] *The New York Times*, Obituary.... December 27, 1903.

[48] *Hagerstown Mail*, February 13, 1829. Also Musey, *It Happened in Washington County*..., p. 55.

[49] Musey, *It Happened...*, p. 55.

[50] *Hagerstown Mail*, February 13, 1829.

[51] This unnamed newspaper article was quoted by Thomas J.C. Williams, *History of Washington County*..., p. 195.

[52] *Hagerstown Mail*, February 13, 1829.

[53] Musey, *It Happened...*, p. 55.

[54] J.M. Carper, Email to the author; August 3, 2009.

[55] *Frederick-Town Herald*, February 14, 1829.

[56] Letter to the author; Frederick County Public Libraries, ud, 2009.

[57] *Frederick-Town Herald*, February 14, 1829.

[58] Jacob Engelbrecht, *Diary entry*, February 9, 1829. The author is grateful to Mary Mannix of the Frederick County Public Libraries for making this diary available.

[59] Robert V. Remini, *Andrew Jackson and the Course of American Freedom 1822-1832* (New York: Harper, 1981), p. 159.

[60] *Easton Gazette* (Easton, Maryland), February 14, 1829.

[61] Ibid.

[62] *United States Telegraph*, February 12, 1829.

[63] *Aurora & Pennsylvania Gazette* (Philadelphia, PA), February 14, 1829.

[64] *Newport Mercury* (Newport, RI), February 14, 1829; *Easton Gazette* (Easton, MD), February 14, 1829; *Farmer's Cabinet* (Amherst, NH), February 14, 1829.

[65] *Richmond Enquirer* (Richmond, VA), January 27, 1829.

[66] Ibid. Also *Baltimore Gazette and Daily Advertiser* (Baltimore, MD), January 23, 1829.

[67] *Richmond Enquirer* (Richmond, VA), February 14, 1829. Also *United States' Telegraph* (Washington,D.C.), February 12, 1829.

[68] Remini, *Andrew Jackson...*, p. 159.

[69] Ibid.

[70] For a description of this procedure, see *Mechanics' Free Press* (Philadelphia, PA) February 21, 1829. See also *Hagerstown Mail* (Hagerstown, MD), February 13, 1829, and *The Newport Mercury* (Newport, RI), February 14, 1829.

[71] The speeches on this occasion were printed in the *Adams Sentinel* (Gettysburg, PA), February 11, 1829.

[72] Ibid.

[73] Ibid.

[74] *Daily Gazette* (Cincinnati, OH), March 4, 1829.

[75] Ibid.

[76] William W. Story (ed) *Life and Letters of Joseph Story*, v 1 (Freeport, NY, Books for Libraries Press, 1971), p. 563.

Chapter 11, Coming Home

[1] Marquis James, *The Life of Andrew Jackson: Portrait of a President*, (New York: Garden City Publishing co., Inc., 1940), p. 495. See also Jon Meacham, *American Lion: Andrew Jackson in the White House* (New York: Random House, 2008), p. 61.

[2] *New Hampshire Patriot and State Gazette; March 20, 1837.*

[3] Ibid.

[4] Ibid.

[5] Ibid.

[6] Marquis James, *The Life of Andrew Jackson...*, p. 724.

[7] Ibid. Some newspapers made light of Van Buren's issue of an Executive Order for the Surgeon General to accompany ex-President Jackson on his homeward journey. This Executive Order included a provision that the Assistant Surgeon General of the United States, General Reynolds, join the party at Wheeling and go on to the Hermitage with Jackson. One newspaper editorialized: "To effect this simple operation a pompous General Order has been issued, signed by Mr. Van Buren himself, as Commander in Chief and

countersigned by the Secretary of War, and the Adjutant General in the name of Major Gen. McComb." See *Farmer's Cabinet*, March 17, 1837. Another newspaper ,however, defended Van Buren's General Order. "This mark of affection on the part of the President to his infirm and venerable predecessor was peculiarly necessary under the circumstances, and will excite much general satisfaction throughout the country." *Jamestown Journal*, (NY), March 22, 1837.

[8] A recent biography, though, says Jackson left on March 7, 1837. See Jon Meacham, *American Lion: Andrew Jackson in the White House* (New York: Random House, 2008), p. 340.

[9] James, *The Life of Andrew Jackson...*, p. 724.

[10] Daniel Walker Howe, *What Hath God Wrought: The Transformation of America, 1815-1848* (New York: Oxford University Press, 2007), p. 563.

[11] *Eastern Argus* (Portland, ME); March 14, 1837.

[12] *Jamestown Journal* (NY), March 22, 1837.

[13] Marquis James, *The Life of Andrew Jackson....*, p. 724.

[14] *Journal of Commerce* (Washington, D.C.), March 7, 1837.

[15] *Patriot and Democrat* (Hartford, CT), March 18, 1837.

[16] H. W. Brands, *Andrew Jackson: His Life and Times* (New York: Anchor Books, 2004), p. 532. See also John S. Jenkins, *The Life of Andrew Jackson, Seventh President of the United States* (Buffalo, NY: Derby & Newsome, 1847), p. 186.

[17] Unfortunately, the newspapers of the day did not define this "indisposition." In all likelihood, it was another attack of severe gastrointestinal problems. See *National Gazette and Literary Register* (Philadelphia, PA), March 18, 1837. Other famous guests at the Highland Hall Hotel in Frostburg included—over the years— Thomas Hart Benton, Davy Crockett, Sam Houston, Zachary Taylor, Lewis Cass and Frosburg's "local favorite" and Jackson's old enemy, Henry Clay. When the section of the Baltimore and Ohio Railroad was completed from Cumberland, Maryland, to Wheeling, Virginia, it cut off the winter trade at the Highland Hall. It was sold in 1853 to the Catholic Church, and was remodeled into a church. A replacement church still sits (2011) on the site of the old Highland Hall Hotel. The author is indebted to Professor David Dean of Frostburg State University for this information.

[18] *Pittsfield Sun* (MA) March 30, 1837.

[19] *New Bedford Mercury* (RI), March 17, 1837. Also the *New York Spectator* (NY), March 24, 1837.

[20] *Pittsfield Sun*, March 30, 1837.

[21] Letter, J. Cunningham to Reuben Lewis; April 9, 1837. Virginia Historical Society (VIH Mss 2C9175a1); Richmond, Virginia. See also Jon Meacham, *Andrew Jackson: American Lion* (New York: Random House, 2008), p. 441.

[22] One biographer wrote that Jackson spent a "fortnight" in Cincinnati, visiting many of his friends there See Augustus C. Buell *History of Andrew Jackson* (New York: Scribners, 1904), p. 366. This claim is not likely; if Jackson left Washington on March 6 and arrived in Nashville on March 25, he could not have stopped anywhere for lengthy periods of time.

[23] Cunningham Letter.

[24] Ibid.

[25] Ibid.

[26] *Lowell Patriot* (MA), April 4, 1837.

[27] Ibid.

[28] One newspaper apparently wanted to dampen all this enthusiasm for Jackson's return. The *Nashville Banner* said the greetings were "the smallest we recollect ever to have seen on any public occasion when he was the object. So much for making himself the head of a party instead of the President of a nation." Quoted in *Pennsylvania Engineer*, April 10, 1837.

[29] Marsha Mullin, Email to the author, January, 2010. The highly decorative sarcophagus is on display at the Smithsonian Institution in Washington, D.C.

[30] Matthew Warshauer, "Ridiculing the Dead: Andrew Jackson and Connecticut Newspapers," *Connecticut History*, 40 (1), p. 107. Other cities that sponsored "sham" or "mock" funerals included Washington, D.C., Philadelphia, Boston, Richmond, Nashville, Pottsville, Pennsylvania; and Frederick, Maryland.

[31] Matthew Warshauer, "Contested Mourning: The New York Battle over Andrew Jackson's Death," *New York History*, Winter, 2006, p. 29.

[32] Warshauer, "Ridiculing the Dead...," p. 106.

33 Ibid.

34 Apparently, the news of his death was sent out by telegraph.

35 This account of Louisville's "sham" Jackson funeral, was taken from notes of Alfred Pirtle in the Pirtle Papers, BI F4896 115; Filson Society, Louisville, Kentucky.

36 Ibid.

ACKNOWLEDGMENTS

All authors know that in researching and writing a book, they must have help from many different sources. This book is certainly no exception. I have so many people to thank that I am a bit reluctant to mention any, lest I omit some. Good manners, however, require me—as much as I possibly can—to acknowledge the great amounts of assistance I have received in preparation of this book.

I wish to mention first the two graduate assistants at Western Kentucky University who were vital to the successful completion of this work: Thomas Lee Anderson and David Kerr were always on hand to run down sources and give me advice when I needed it. The Research Committee at WKU granted funds which allowed necessary travel; I thank, especially, Dr. Phil Myers, Lindsay Sullivan, and Molly Swietek, for helping me with this grant.

No author would get very far without good libraries and excellent librarians. I am proud to say that WKU has some of the best librarians in the country. Nancy Richey, as always, was extremely helpful in guiding me to various sources, as was Nancy Baird. The Interlibrary Loan Department at WKU, headed by Selina Langford, kept me supplied with necessary books and magazine articles. Marsha Skipworth, History Department Secretary, was helpful in many ways, as was Department Chairman, Robert Dietle, whose help and encouragement in my publishing endeavors are most appreciated. Professor Debbie Kreitzer of the WKU Geography Department furnished me with useful maps, for which I am grateful. Student assistants Leigh-Ann St. Charles and Chelsea Kastin helped in many significant ways. Glen Connor, Professor at WKU and KY State meteorologist, sent much needed weather information.

Dr. Drew Harrington, Professor of History, of Cumming, Georgia, read the entire manuscript, and suggested numerous improvements, as did Professor Richard Weigel of WKU History

Department. Both Drew and Rich are my friends and colleagues, and I thank them sincerely for helping me with this project.

I wish also to thank the staffs of The Hermitage, particularly Marsha Mullin, for their assistance, as well as the personnel at the Tennessee Historical Society in Nashville, and the Filson Society in Louisville. I owe a tremendous debt of gratitude to Diann Benti and Ashley Cataldo, both of the American Antiquarian Society in Worcester, Massachusetts, for finding relevant newspaper and magazine articles.

While this work was in progress, I wrote letters to numerous newspapers in the towns and cities through which Jackson passed in 1829. I wanted to know if there were any "passed-down" stories from one generation to another, about the time the President-elect visited. I also wrote numerous emails to individuals who know about steamboats, coaches, railroads, and Andrew Jackson. With both the newspaper and Email appeals, the results were gratifying. I wish, therefore, to thank the following people for their help and encouragement:

Susan Abbott, Michael Alderson, N. Anders, Judy Asman, Jonathan Atkins, Bob Barrows, Debra Basham, Alan Bates, Rick Bell, Joseph Berger, H.W. Brands, Cassie Bratcher, Jill Byers, Betsy Caldwell, Gay Campbell, G.S. Clarke, J.M. Carper (who sent much useful material from Hagerstown, MD); Barry Chad, Richard E. Clem, David Dean, Brenda Dickson, Marvin Downing, Jennifer Duplaga, Inge Dupont, Melissa Earnest, Gail Farr, George Fetherling, John Finger, Kevin Fredette, John Fryant, Judy Fugate, Robert Garver, Jill Godlewski, John Goldsmith, Susan Gordon, Eric Green, Jerry E. Green, Sarah-Elizabeth Gundlach, Megin Harrington, Jeff Harris, Tommy Hines, Jim Holmberg, Roberta Hood, Edward J. Hopkins, Mary E. Johnson, Bill Judd, Tom Kanon, Tara Laver, Greg Lambousy, Russ Lampkins (who supplied me with much needed river data); Thomas Lannon, Bill Larson, Jacob Lee, Karl Lietzenmayer, Deborah Liptak, C. Arthur Louderback, Elizabeth Mahoney, John Marszalek, Lyn Martin, Jan Mueller, Edward Muller, Nori Muster, Catherine Osborne, Edward A. Owens, Charles "Chuck" Parrish, Diana Patterson, Wendy Pflug, Sara Jane Poindexter, Elizabeth Pope,. Robert Remini, Randall

Rubell, Barbara Rust, John Seigenthaler, Linda Showalter, David Smith, Ray Swick, Jeanne Sugg, Benjamin Terpstra, Marc Thomas, Ann Toplovich, Joe Trotter, Harold Vann, Andy Verhoff, Thea Walsh, Matthew Warshauer, John White, Sean Wilentz, Michael L. Wilhelm, Katherine Wilkins, Eleanor Williams, Howard Winn, Steve Wiser, William M. Worden, Jessica Zele, and Dan Zyglowicz.

I thank, too, my publisher, Doug Sikes, for his continued support of my literary endeavors. And finally, I wish to extend my gratitude to my family, for their forbearance while this book was in progress: daughters, Beverly and Hilary; sons, Daniel and Matthew; and granddaughters, Colleen, Megan, Katharine, Gwynnen Mindora; grandsons, Travis, Patrick, Austin, Liam, Rowan, Oliver, Henry, Cranley, and Isaac; and David Daniel, Finn, and Kellan. And to Ling and Elaine and to Steve and Arthur. And, first, foremost, and always, Pat.

BIBLIOGRAPHY

Adams Sentinel (Gettysburg,PA); February 11, 1829.

American Friend and Marietta Gazette (OH); January 10, 1829; February 21, 1829.

American Repertory (St. Albans, PA); January 29, 1829.

Argus of Western America; January 28, 1829.

Augusta Chronicle and Georgia Advertiser (GA); February 11, 1829; February 11, 1829.

Aurora and Pennsylvania Gazette (Philadelphia); February 10, 1829.

Baltimore Gazette and Daily Advertiser; January 30, 1829.

Baltimore Patriot (MD), February 3, 1829; February 10, 1829.

Banner-Whig (Nashville, TN); December 27, 1828; January 3, 1829.

Beach, Ursula Smith. *Along the Warioto, or a History of Montgomery County, Tennessee.* Clarksville, TN, 1964.

Beall-Booth Family Letters; AB 365 52,66,68; Filson Club; Louisville, KY.

Berryman, Carrie Ann, "Foklore and Historic Research Concerning the Gower House," Paper, Murray State University, 1997, pp. 2-15.

Brands, H. W. *Andrew Jackson: His Life and Times.* New York: Anchor Books, 2004.

Buell, Augustus C. *History of Andrew Jackson.* New York: Scribners, 1904.

Bumgarner, John R. *The Health of the Presidents: The 41 United States Presidents Through 1993 From a Physician's Point of View.* Jefferson, NC: McFarland Press, 1994.

Burke, Pauline Wilcox. *Emily Donelson of Tennessee*. Richmond, VA: Garret and Massie.

Cadet and Statesman (Providence, RI); February 2, 1829; February 7, 1829.

Caldwell, J. A. *History of Belmont and Jefferson Counties*. Wheeling, WVA: The Historical Society, nd.

Carolina Observer (Fayetteville, NC); February 5, 1829.

Carper, J. M. Email to the author; August 3, 2009.

Cheathem, Mark R. *Old Hickory's Nephew: The Political and Private Struggles of Andrew Jackson Donelson*. Baton Rouge: LSU Press, 2007.

Cincinnati Chronicle (OH); January 18, 1829; January 31, 1829; March 14, 1829.

Cincinnati Gazette (OH); August 29, 1828; October 21, 1828; February 11, 1829.

Connecticut Mirror; February 14, 1829.

Connor, Glenn. Weather Notes for 1829.

Cooper, James Fenimore. *Home as Found*. New York: The Co-Operative Publication Society, 1884.

Cothron, Tracy, "Smithland: Through the Windows of the Gower House," Smithland, KY: Livingston County Historical Society, pp. 1-10.

"Crawford-Hutchinson," Smithland, KY: Livingston County, Historical Society, np.

Cummings, Samuel. *The Western Pilot*. Cincinnati: SYN and Guilford, 1833.

Daily Gazette (Cincinnati, OH); March 4, 1829.

Douglas, Byrd. *Steamboatin' on the Cumberland*. Nashville: Tennessee Book Co., 1961.

Dunbar, Seymour. *History of Travel*, v II. Indianapolis: Bobbs-Merrill, 1915.

Dunglison, Robley. *A Dictionary of American Science 11th ed.* Philadelphia: Blanchard and Lea, 1854.

Eastern Argus (Portland, ME); March 22, 1837.

Easton Gazette (MD); February 14, 1829.

Engelbrecht, Jacob. *Diary*. Frederick County Public Library.

Farmer's Cabinet. (Amherst, NH); January 28, 1829; February 7, 1829; February 14, 1829; March 17, 1837.

Fetherling, George. Email to the author, January 25, 2009.

Fetherling, George. *Wheeling: A Short History*. Wheeling: Polyhedron Learning Media, Inc., 2008.

Francis, Mary C. *A Son of Destiny: The Story of Andrew Jackson*. New York: The Federal Book Company, 1902.

Frederick-Town Herald (MD); February 14, 1829.

Gazette and Literary Register (Philadelphia, PA); March 18, 1837.

Goodwin, Philo A. *Biography of Andrew Jackson, President of the United States.* New York: R. Hart Towner, 1833.

Hagerstown Mail (MD); February 6, 1829; February 13, 1829.

Hartford Times (CT); February 16, 1829.

Heilenman, Diane, "Boys of Bourbon: The Love Behind the Labels," *The Courier-Journal* (Louisville, KY), May 3, 2009.

Heiskell, S. G. *Andrew Jackson and Early Tennessee History*, v 1. Nashville: Ambrose Printing Company, 1920.

Home Page, Century Inn; PA.

Horn, Stanley F. *The Hermitage: Home of Old Hickory*. Richmond, VA: Garrett & Massie, 1938.

Howe, Daniel Walker. *What Hath God Wrought: The Transformation of America, 1815-1848*. New York: Oxford University Press, 2007.

Hurt, R. Douglas. *The Ohio Frontier: Crucible of the Old Northwest, 1729-1830*. Bloomington: Indiana University Press, 1998.

Jackson, Carlton. "Another Place, Another Time: The Attempted Assassination of Andrew Jackson," *Tennessee Historical Quarterly*, 26 (Summer, 1967), pp. 184-190.

Jackson, Carlton. *Presidential Vetoes, 1792-1945*. Athens: The University of Georgia Press, 1967.

Jackson, Carlton. *Zane Grey*. Boston: Twayne Publishers, 1973.

James, Marquis. *The Life of Andrew Jackson: Portrait of a President*. New York: Garden City Publishing Company, 1940.

Jefferson, Josephine. *Wheeling Glass*. Mt. Vernon, OH: Guide Publications, 1947.

Jenkins, *The Life of Andrew Jackson, Seventh President of the United States*. Buffalo, NY: Derby & Newsome, 1847.

Johnson, Gerald W. *Andrew Jackson: An Epic in Homespun*. New York: Minton, Balch& Co., 1927.

Journal of Commerce (Washington, D.C.); March 7, 1837.

Kleber, John E. et al (eds). *The Encyclopedia of Louisville*. Lexington: The University Press of Kentucky, 2001.

Knoxville Register (TN); December 31, 1828.

Krull, Kathleeen and Kathryn Hewitt. *Lives of the Presidents: Fame, Shame (And What the Neighbors Thought)*. New York: Harcourt-Brace, 1998.

Letter, Andrew Jackson to Katherine Duane Morgan; January 3, 1829. *Andrew Jackson Papers*, v VII. Knoxville: University of Tennessee Press, 1961.

Letter, Andrew Jackson to James Ronaldson, January 4, 1828. *Papers of Andrew Jackson v vII*. Knoxville: University of Tennessee Press, 2007.

Letter, Andrew Jackson to Richard Call; December 22, 1828. *Andrew Jackson Papers*, v VII. Knoxville: The University of Tennessee Press, 1961.

Letter, Charles Coffin to Andrew Jackson; January 21, 1829.

Papers of Andrew Jackson v VII. Knoxville: The University of Tennessee Press, 2007.

Letter, J. Cunningham to Reuben Lewis; April 9, 1837. Virginia Historical Society, VIH Mss 2C9175a1.

Letter, Ezra Stiles Ely to Andrew Jackson; January 28, 1829. Bassett, John Spencer, *Correspondence of Andrew Jackson*. Washington, D.C..Carnegie Institute, 1902.

Letter, Lyman Beecher to Ezra Stiles; January 20, 1829. Bassett, John Spencer, *Correspondence of Andrew Jackson*. Washington, D.C.: Carnegie Institute, 1902.

Letter, Rachel Jackson to Louise Moreau Davezec de Lassy Livingston; December 1, 1828. *Papers of Andrew Jackson*. Knoxville: University of Tennessee Press, 1961.

Letter, Robert Punshon to Andrew Jackson; February 6, 1829. The Papers of Andrew Jackson, v vii, 1829. Knoxville: University of Tennessee Press, 2007.

Letter to the Author; Frederick County Public Libraries, nd., 2009.

Louisville Public Advertiser (KY); January 21, 1829; January 24, 1829; February 7, 1829.

Lowell Patriot (MA); April 4, 1837.

McCague, James. *The Cumberland*. New York: Holt, Rinehart and Winston, 1973.

Maryland Gazette (Annapolis), February 5, 1829.

Mason Lodge No. 60, Brownsville, PA. Minutes, February 2, 1829.

Meacham, Jon. *American Lion: Andrew Jackson in the White House*. New York: Random House, 2008.

Merchant Steam Vessels of the United States, 1790-1868. Providence, RI: Steamship Society, 2009.

Moser, Harold. "Andrew Jackson, 1767-1845," *The Tennessee Historical Encyclopedia of History and Culture* (Knoxville:

University of Tennessee Press,2002).http://tennessee encyclopedia.net/imagegalley.php?Entry id=J005.

Mullin, Marsha. Email to the author; January, 2010.

Musey, Ruben. *It Happened in Washington County*. Hagerstown, MD:Washington County Bicentennial Committee, 1976.

New Bedford Mercury (RI); March 17, 1837.

New Hampshire Patriot and State Gazette; January 26, 1829; February 10, 1829; March 20, 1837.

Newport Mercury (RI); February 14, 1829.

New York Spectator, March 24, 1837.

Nicholson, Meredith. *The Cavalier of Tennessee*. Indianapolis: IN, 1928.

Norwich Courier (CT); February 4, 1829.

Norwich Republican (VA); February 4, 1829.

Oxford English Dictionary, compact, 2ed. Oxford, England: Clarendon Press, 1989.

Parton, James. *Life of Andrew Jackson, v III*. New York: Mason Brothers, 1860.

Patriot and Democrat (Hartford, CT); March 18, 1837.

Pennsylvania Engineer, April 10, 1837.

Phillips, Jimmy, "My Connection to the 7th President of the United States," Pamphlet; Smithland, KY: Livingston County Historical Society, nd.

Pirtle, Alfred. Collection, Pirtle Papers BI F4896 115; Filson Society; Louisville, KY.

Pittsburgh Mercury, February 9, 1829.

Pittsfield Sun (MA); March 30, 1837.

Portland Advertiser and Gazette of Maine (Portland, ME); February 2, 1829; February 6, 1829.

Raitz, Karl (ed). *The National Road*. Baltimore: The John Hopkins Press, 1996.

Remini, Robert. *Andrew Jackson and the Course of American Freedom 1822-1832. New York: Harper, 1981.*

Richmond Enquirer (VA); January 27, 1829; January 29, 1829; February 10, 1829; February 14, 1829.

Salem Gazette (MA); February 3, 1829; March 2, 1829.

Schlesinger, Arthur M., Jr. *The Age of Jackson.* Boston: Little, Brown & Co., 1945.

Sentinel and Witness (Middletown, CT); February 11, 1829.

Sharkey, John. *Travel Diary, July 16-29.* Filson Club, A S 5 3 1, Louisville, KY.

Shawneetown Gazette (IL); January 24, 1829.

Story, William W. (ed). *Life and Letters of Joseph Story,* v 1. Freeport, NY: Books for Libraries Press, 1971.

Tarkington, Booth. *The Magnificent Ambersons* Glouceser, Mass: Peter Smith, 1967.

The Daily News Standard (Uniontown, PA); November 21, 1829.

The Genuis (Uniontown,PA); February 4, 1829.

The New York Commercial, November 1, 1828.

The New York Times, December 27, 1903.

The Scioto Gazette (OH), February 4, 1829.

Trollope, Frances. *Domestic Manners of the Americans.* New York: Knopf, 1949.

United States Telegraph; January 26, 1829; February 2, 1829; February 9, 1829; February 12, 1829.

Vecchione, Glen. *The Little Giant Book of American Presidents.* New York: Sterling, 2007.

Vermont Gazette (Bennington, VT); February 3, 1829.

Vermont Patriot and State Gazette (Montpelier); February 9, 1829.

Virginia Statesman; January 28, 1829.

Warshauer, Matthew, "Contested Mourning: The New York Battle Over Andrew Jackson's Death," *New York History*, Winter, 2006, pp. 29-65.

Warshauer, Matthew, "Ridiculing the Dead: Andrew Jackson and Connecticut Newspapers," *Connecticut History*, 40 (l), pp.101-119,

Wheeling's First 250 Years: Short History done in Celebration of Service to Our Neighbors in Wheeling for half that Period, 1817-1942. Wheeling: The National Bank of West Virginia,1942.

Wheeling Gazette, January 31, 1829.

White, John H. *Steamboats on the Inland Rivers.* Oxford, OH: The Walter Havinghurst Special Collections, nd.

Williams, Thomas J. C. *History of Washington County, Maryland, From the Earliest Settlements to the Present Time*, v. 1. Clearfield Company and Family Line Publications, 1992.

Yater, George W. *Two Hundred Years at the Falls of the Ohio: A History of Louisville and Jefferson County*. Louisville, KY: The Heritage Corporation of Louisville and Jefferson County, 1979.

ABOUT THE AUTHOR

Carlton Jackson is a University Distinguished Professor of History at Western Kentucky University in Bowling Green, KY, where he has taught since 1961. He was also the University's first Right Honorable Mace.

He has served as a Visiting Professor at the College of William and Mary in Williamsburg, VA; Tufts University in Medford, MA; the University of Hawaii in Honolulu, Hawaii; Graz University in Austria; and Belize College in Belize.

He has had four senior lecture Fulbright awards to India, Pakistan, Bangladesh, and in the 1989-90 school year was the Bicentennial Professor of American Studies at the University of Helsinki.

He lives with his wife, Pat, in Butler County, Kentucky. He is the author of several books, including *Joseph Gavi: Young Hero of the Minsk Ghetto*, also published by Acclaim Press.

INDEX

189

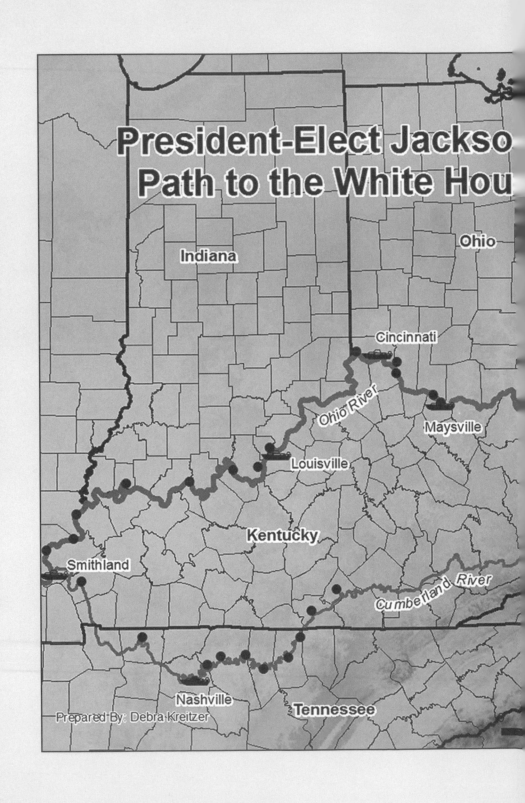